The
Christian
Mind

The Christian Mind

How should
a Christian think?

Harry Blamires

REGENT COLLEGE PUBLISHING
Vancouver, British Columbia

The Christian Mind
Copyright © 1963 Harry Blamires
All rights reserved.

First edition 1963 by S.P.C.K.
Holy Trinity Church, Marylebone Road, London

This edition published 2005 by Regent College Publishing
5800 University Boulevard, Vancouver, BC V6T 2E4 Canada
Web: www.regentpublishing.com
E-mail: info@regentpublishing.com

Views expressed in works published by Regent College Publishing are
those of the author and do not necessarily represent the official position
of Regent College <www.regent-college.edu>.

Library and Archives Canada Cataloguing in Publication Data

Blamires, Harry
    The Christian mind : how should a Christian think / Harry Blamires.

Originally published: London : S.P.C.K., 1963.
Includes bibliographical references.
ISBN 1-57383-323-1

    1. Christian life—Anglican authors. 2. Christianity and culture.
3. Secularism. I. Title.

BV4501.2.B546 2005   230

C2005-900524-6

CONTENTS

PREFACE TO THE REGENT EDITION

O N THE DAY when I decided to write this book I had heard someone speak of 'the scientific mind' and someone else of 'the modern mind', using the word *mind* of a collectively accepted set of notions and attitudes. Surely, I thought, there was, or there ought to be, a definable 'Christian mind'. After all, as we Christians talked with others, as we read our newspapers or listened to the media, we were continually thinking, or ought to be thinking, 'But no, that's not the way we Christians look at things'. So I set about the task of illustrating how truly Christian thinking put us on a collision course with contemporary secularist assumptions.

Now, forty years later, the basic situation has not changed —except in the sense that the collision between the secularist and Christian presuppositions has intensified. Ought my initial analysis of the collision in terms of the contemporary scene to be updated? I have recently given a lot of thought to this possibility. The trouble is that, if it were so updated, it would quickly 'date' again. The fact that the book has been continuously in print since 1963 suggests that readers do not have difficulty in this respect. Looking back on the polemical books that I read avidly in my youth, I cannot think that I had problems with the then dated element in Chesterton's *Orthodoxy* or *The Everlasting Man*. Would Lewis's *Screwtape Letters* be more acceptable today if the background of the Second World War were changed to that of the struggle with al Qaeda?

The Christian Mind was enthusiastically reviewed. It was published just a few weeks after John Robinson's *Honest to God* had shaken the theological world. This coincidence proved crucial in two ways, helpful and unhelpful. The helpful aspect was that many believers who had been repelled by the bishop's book flocked to buy and to recommend my book as a counterbalancing 'blast from orthodoxy', to quote one reviewer. The unhelpful consequence was that it encouraged hostile liberals to characterise me as the hidebound enemy of new thinking. Moreover, cast in the role of the man who had taken on John Robinson, I found myself in a rather absurd position. People who organized courses and were looking for speakers seemed to assume that that my book constituted some kind of conscious 'reply' to a book whose publication preceded it by only three weeks.

My next book *A Defence of Dogmatism* (in the USA called *The Tyranny of Time*) came out in 1965. In it I sought to demythologise secularism by encouraging scepticism about the framework of assumptions within which fashionable thinking denigrated the religious. A more difficult book and therefore little noticed, it represented a farewell to theological writing for some fifteen years. C. S. Lewis had told me that I ought to write in my own field, indeed that it was a way of drawing attention to my specifically Christian output. And any way, being professionally employed in the field of English Literature, I felt the need to refresh my work.

It was in the USA that interest in my early theological books revived. James Manney of Servant Publications, Ann Arbor, arranged the reissue of *The Christian Mind* in 1978 and the publication of *Where do we stand?* in 1980. Having taken early retirement from the academic world in 1976, I was in a position to continue work in both the literary and the theological fields and I enjoyed successive lecturing trips to the USA and to Canada in the following decade. My simple guide to Christian teaching (*On Christian Truth*) came out in 1983 and my critique of our current situation (*The Post-Christian Mind*) was written for the millennium. I am very grateful to Rob Clements for the decision to give a new lease of life to several of my books.

PART ONE

The Lack of a Christian Mind

1

THE SURRENDER TO SECULARISM

THERE IS no longer a Christian mind. It is a commonplace that the mind of modern man has been secularized. For instance, it has been deprived of any orientation towards the supernatural. Tragic as this fact is, it would not be so desperately tragic had the Christian mind held out against the secular drift. But unfortunately the Christian mind has succumbed to the secular drift with a degree of weakness and nervelessness unmatched in Christian history. It is difficult to do justice in words to the complete loss of intellectual morale in the twentieth-century Church. One cannot characterize it without having recourse to language which will sound hysterical and melodramatic.

There is no longer a Christian mind. There is still, of course, a Christian ethic, a Christian practice, and a Christian spirituality. As a moral being, the modern Christian subscribes to a code other than that of the non-Christian. As a member of the Church, he undertakes obligations and observations ignored by the non-Christian. As a spiritual being, in prayer and meditation, he strives to cultivate a dimension of life unexplored by the non-Christian. But as a *thinking* being, the modern Christian has succumbed to secularization. He accepts religion—its morality, its worship, its spiritual culture; but he rejects the religious view of life, the view which

3

sets all earthly issues within the context of the eternal, the view which relates all human problems—social, political, cultural—to the doctrinal foundations of the Christian Faith, the view which sees all things here below in terms of God's supremacy and earth's transitoriness, in terms of Heaven and Hell.

Everywhere one meets examples of the Church's abdication of intellectual authority which lies at the back of the modern Christian's easy descent into mental secularism. A few weeks ago, in the chapel of a Church training college, I heard a bishop impress upon his congregation that Church colleges do not exist to give Church teaching but rather to provide opportunities for communal worship. This false antithesis, with all its dangerous implications, was pressed home. The duty of common worship was urged with all the force of episcopal authority. With the same authority the significance of doctrinal teaching was depreciated. A passing reference to the evil materialistic idolatries prevalent to-day completed a neat circuit of error and illogicality.

Of course when one speaks of the loss of intellectual morale in the twentieth-century Church one has in mind much more than the depreciation of the doctrinal demand by unthinking ecclesiastics. My thesis amounts to this. Except over a very narrow field of thinking, chiefly touching questions of strictly personal conduct, we Christians in the modern world accept, for the purpose of mental activity, a frame of reference constructed by the secular mind and a set of criteria reflecting secular evaluations. There is no Christian mind; there is no shared field of discourse in which we can move at ease as thinking Christians by trodden ways and past established landmarks.

4

THE SURRENDER TO SECULARISM

Perhaps most of the acclaimed thinkers and prophets of our day are non-Christians. A glance at some of the influential critiques of our culture that have made a popular impact in the last few years would suggest this view. Many writers who have recently probed the values of our culture, scrutinized the quality of current civilization with critical and penetrating eyes, have done so from a humanistic standpoint. Consider, for instance, Jacques Barzun's discerning analysis of modern educational error and delusion in *The House of Intellect*, or, at a more popular level, the exposure of the corruptions of our social and commercial life in Vance Packard's books (*The Hidden Persuaders* and *The Status-Seekers*). Consider W. H. Whyte's book, *The Organisation Man*, which provides an ironic and devastating study of the new image of ideal manhood now being cultivated by the mechanized society of the industrial West, an ideal on which generations of men are at this time being nourished, an ideal which appeals wholly to the crude desire to get on in the world. Or, to turn from the American to the British scene, consider the work of our own critics of contemporary culture, such as Raymond Williams (*Culture and Society*), Richard Hoggart (*The Uses of Literacy*), and Martin Green (*A Mirror for Anglo-Saxons*). And these books are listed, not because they are necessarily profound, but because they represent a vital and influential current in the thinking and talking of to-day.

There are two points to be made about the work of fashionable sociological writers. In the first place, though many of their books reflect a deep concern and unease over the present state of our culture and brood critically upon the sham values which commerce is imposing on modern man, generally speaking the

5

judgements passed are not Christian judgements. They are not the products of Christian insight, Christian instruction, Christian vision. No theology lies at the back of what is otherwise an apparently healthy rejection of current materialism in its cruder manifestations. Whatever the private beliefs of the writers I have mentioned may be, their books cannot be said to bring the religious view of life to bear upon the human scene.

The second point to be stressed here is that critics of contemporary culture such as those I have mentioned, taking their stand on a humanistic basis, are all contributing to a living dialogue. This dialogue is being carried on in our midst, a feature of our intellectual life. It presses immediately upon us. It threads its way through our lives if our lot is cast among men of intelligence. It is intertwined with our friendships and meets us in quiet reflective moments as we take up a book in the bookshop or the library, or pick up a week-end journal in the home. The stream of talk among thinking people to-day presupposes a knowledge of the rigorous critique to which humanism is subjecting contemporary civilization. Write a critical condemnation of modern man for his enslavement to the machine, to the advertisers, to the image-makers, the monopolists, the bureaucrats; throw in a few acknowledgements to D. H. Lawrence, George Orwell, or even Matthew Arnold; and you will straightway find yourself at home and at ease among garrulous companions in a well-populated field of discourse. For the books I have mentioned show the modern mind at work on its prophetic side. They are born of the secular mind and in turn they nourish the secular mind. They sell in thousands because they fall naturally and easily, upon publication, into a living field of discourse.

6

THE SURRENDER TO SECULARISM

Now consider by contrast the position of, say, Joseph Pieper's book, *Leisure the Basis of Culture*, one of the most interesting and profound attempts in post-war years to reflect critically yet christianly on vital aspects of contemporary culture. It was written in 1947. It was translated into English and issued here in 1952 (thanks to T. S. Eliot). So far as I know, it is still in its first edition. My complaint is not that Packard and Whyte and Hoggart are names widely known while Pieper is popularly unknown — though that is unfortunately true. Nor is it that even Christians themselves are ready to neglect the little-discussed Pieper, but not to put themselves out of the swim by neglecting Packard or Whyte, though again that is sadly true. My point is that there is no immediate living dialogue to which Pieper's work contributes. It does not take its place in a current conversation, the utterance of a readily understood voice adopting a familiar mode of discourse. (One is not of course denying the existence of a larger historical dialogue carried on over the centuries by giants like St Augustine, St Thomas, Kierkegaard, and by Pieper himself.) Without denying the impact of important isolated utterances, one must admit that there is no packed contemporary field of discourse in which writers are reflecting christianly on the modern world and modern man.

I have mentioned Martin Green's recent and much-discussed book, *A Mirror for Anglo-Saxons*. It has, with good reason, played quite a part in the season's talk. It has fed an interesting current into the year's thinking for many people. No doubt there are many clumsinesses in the book, but nevertheless it contains a discerning characterization of the traditional Britishness fostered by many forces in our cultural set-up.

Green makes a bold attempt to distinguish between a genuine and worthy Britishness and the sterile, sham ideal foisted upon generation after generation of our fellow-countrymen through the shallow conformities imposed by our Press, our educational system, our social etiquette, and the forces of publicity. Time after time, in reading this book, one will mentally applaud as some feature of current snobbery, self-deception, vanity, or greed is exposed and probed. Yet it is all done in the name of an ideal which the Christian rejects. The whole analytical process is carried out within a frame of reference which totally excludes the spiritual dimension, which totally ignores man's primary nature as a religious being. The thesis is worked out within a frame of reference whose key human ideal is apparently represented by the odd juxtaposition of D. H. Lawrence, F. R. Leavis, George Orwell, and Kingsley Amis.

Where is the comparable analysis and critique of the false ideal of Britishness which is rooted in Christian evaluations? There is none of course. Publicly the discussion of Green's book has been carried on most notably in the sceptical journals. The thinking Christian has to step in and out of the field of discourse in which current values are thus analysed, like a man putting on and off protective clothing. Joining, as a reader or a conversationalist, in the discussion of the issues which Green has raised, one has to become temporarily—mentally—a non-Christian. Otherwise one carries on a private monologue. This is because, on entering the field of discourse inhabited by Green and his like, one finds one is the only Christian present.

Thus prophetic condemnation of salient features of contemporary secularism comes nowadays from secularists themselves whose ground of judgement is a humanistic one. It is clear that where there is no Christian mind to pass judgement upon society, those who care for human dignity and integrity on other grounds than the Christian's will be provoked to rebel against the multifarious tendencies of contemporary civilization to depersonalize men and women. This rebellion must be regarded as a significant feature of the post-Christian world. It is good in itself. That is to say, the protest needs to be made. What is bad is that it should come from outside the Christian tradition.

In the same way, if we turn to the world of imaginative literature, we shall find that the deepest rejections of the shallowness and shoddiness of twentieth-century civilization are issuing from artists who are utterly out of touch with the Christian tradition. A series of profound and passionate protests against the vulgarities and dishonesties of twentieth-century society has come from gifted and sensitive literary men in the last fifty years. For the most part these protests have represented a human spirit outraged by the indignities heaped upon it, yet knowing nothing of God. The twentieth-century literature of Protest is a moving and searching fruit of human integrity. Yet at the same time it is a monument to the Church's failure to *think*. For surely, if the Church had been thinking, it would have been with these men, upholding them. Instead it has not been on speaking terms with them.

I am not of course thinking now of the over-publicized angry young men. Neither John Osborne nor Colin Wilson has any great talent, and the fame of both will be ephemeral. The great twentieth-century literature of Protest has stemmed from writers much more gifted than these — with imagination, compassion, and self-dedication. The line starts with Kafka. It takes

9

in D. H. Lawrence. If, for purpose of argument, I were to pick out three powerful and representative voices of Protest, I might well name Louis-Ferdinand Céline, Henry Miller, and Samuel Beckett.

The puritan would straightway point out that these three writers have been branded as obscene. By that fact alone perhaps one can measure the tragedy of their alignment against the Church. For each of the three has, in his own way, brought a keen imaginative penetration to bear upon the grotesque griefs and helpless endeavours of twentieth-century man. Each of them has got to grips with man's lostness, his bewilderment, his rootlessness. If you wish to meet, at a level of deep compassion and tenderness, with the soul of modern man, face to face with all the baffling paraphernalia of contemporary civilization, turn to Beckett's novels and to his plays. Nowhere more poignantly yet humorously are we searched out and known. Here, on a knife-edge between laughter and tears, one lives through an aching yet farcical bewilderment which lacks even the clarity of doubt, the rudder of defined uncertainty. For this *angst*, unrealized and unfaced, is no more than a frowning crease on the forehead and a curling smile about the mouth. Yet it is fathoms deeper than the intellectual's crude scepticism or the shallow chop-logic of the discussion group. Here is a bafflement of the soul —an inner cluelessness prior to that state of organized interrogation at which one can ask: "What is the meaning of life? What is the purpose of anything?" Here is a primitive lostness which allows for nothing so confident as a question (for to ask a question is to presuppose a possible answer, a system of logic, a rationale at the back of things). Here one fumbles for the very means of utterance. There is nothing so articulate as doubt.

Beckett's characters do not aspire to the dignity of defeat. You have to know the rules of the game, you have to be aware that it *is* a game, before you can play it and get thoroughly beaten. That is an achievement beyond them.

The pathos of it is overwhelming. All one can say is: Here is twentieth-century man caught with the heart and the pen as only a genius could catch him. This is the thing itself, as Lear observed of Edgar the Bedlamite. And yet, in the very act of grasping it, embracing it, the Christian mind knows that it will not do. It is the finest, tenderest, profoundest thing we have, yet the heart of the mystery is lacking from it.

What, then, is the position of the thinking Christian, face to face with the cultural situation which I have described? As he reads the things worth reading, whether imaginative or polemical, he is continually meeting with accounts of the human situation or with critical analyses of man's current lot, which make him sit up and say: This is profound and penetrating. This represents a deep and wholly human response to present-day life. It is so crucial, fundamental, and illuminating that it cannot be overlooked. It touches me pre-eminently *as a Christian.* Yet this writer is not a Christian. I share his vision for a moment over this issue or that, and the next minute I am jerked back into awareness that he and I are poles apart, separated by a chasm, by a contradiction in our most basic presuppositions. But (and this is the tragedy) the only way I can pursue this vital current of thought further is by more reading of non-Christian literature written by sceptics, and by discussion of it *within the intellectual frame of reference* which these sceptics have manufactured. In short, there is no current Christian dialogue on this topic. There is no Christian conversation which I can enter, bringing this topic or this vision with me.

There is no Christian dialogue in which the issues are being thrashed out that disturb the rebellious artist and the rebellious prophet. Thus the thinking Christian who is concerned over these issues finds himself fitfully and perversely at one with fiercely—and even blasphemously—non-Christian writers and, at the same time, mentally out of touch with his fellow-Christians. And he scarcely dares to say (how difficult it is to clinch the thing in words anyway) exactly what it is, hidden away among the rabid obscenities of a Henry Miller or the irritable resentments of a Martin Green, which hits him in the eye and searches him out, not just as a man but as a Christian.

As a last example in this particular context, one may cite the problem of totalitarianism. Here is a topic which has produced a great bulk of literature, both polemical and imaginative. A living dialogue is carried on in our midst on this obsessive issue. But it is not a Christian dialogue. It is almost wholly dominated by a concept of freedom whose roots are deep in pagan naturalism. The Christian concept of freedom, rooted as it is in the notion of total self-surrender within the family of God, and accompanied as it is by a code of disciplines rigorous in their check upon self-indulgence or self-assertive individualism, is a virtually contradictory concept to that humanist notion of freedom as residing in an unfettered autonomous individualism, which plagues current thinking to-day. We sense deeply the chasm between the Church and the secular world when those secularists who speak idealistically of freedom reveal that they have in mind, not just the renunciation of dictatorships and other repressive agencies, but

12

also the rejection of bonds and obligations such as those constituted by marriage, the family, and all social hierarchies.

Thus we note with sadness that the twentieth-century works of imaginative literature which have most powerfully nourished man's deep rejection of totalitarianism and most poignantly reflected his suffering under it, have been the products again of non-Christian minds. One thinks, obviously, of George Orwell's *1984*, of Albert Camus's *The Plague*, and of that devastating book from Poland, *The Inquisitors* by George Andrzeyevski. These are books that will continue to represent the thought and experience of our age when we are all forgotten. And two of these ignore, while the third utterly discredits, the religious view of life. Is there in the first rank of anti-totalitarian imaginative literature a work which shows man as the child of God?

We have argued that to-day there is no public pool of discourse fed by christianly committed thought on the world we live in. This deficiency has been illustrated by reference to books: it might equally well have been illustrated by reference to radio or the Press. The deficiency has its effect on the private life of the Christian. Along with other factors in the contemporary situation (such as the rigid class-structure of our society), it has helped to produce the incommunicative congregation characteristic of "fashionable" middle-class parishes especially. If Christians cannot communicate as thinking beings, they are reduced to encountering one another only at the shallow level of gossip and small talk. Hence the perhaps peculiarly modern problem — the loneliness of the thinking Christian. Anyone who

13

wishes to experience this loneliness should try the following experiment. Take some topic of current political importance. Try to establish in your own mind what is the right policy to recommend in relation to it; and do so in total detachment from any political alignment or prejudice; form your conclusions by thinking christianly. Then discuss the matter with fellow-members of your congregation. The full loneliness of the thinking Christian will descend upon you. It is not that people disagree with you. (Some do and some don't.) In a sense that does not matter. But they will not think christianly. They will think pragmatically, politically, but not christianly. In almost all cases you will find that views are wholly determined by political allegiance. Though he does not face it, the loyalty of the average Churchman to the Conservative Party or to the Labour Party is in practical political matters prior to his loyalty to the Church.

It is important that this point about the loneliness of the thinking Christian should not be misunderstood. It is not lonely to disagree with other people. It is not lonely to meet in the same field of discourse with men and women who reach conclusions that contradict your own. But it is desperately lonely to occupy a field of discourse which no one else will enter, even if you are surrounded by people who have reached exactly the same conclusions as you yourself. This is a crucial aspect of the thinking Christian's dilemma in the modern world.

Let me illustrate this point with a personal recollection. I have taught for many years in a Church training college. Several years ago a senior man from the Ministry of Education (now retired) came down to the college in order to recommend (to use a polite euphemism for "impose") a change in policy and practice with particular reference to the training of teachers for work in junior schools. The change was to bring the college course into line with the extreme movement (now discredited) for further weakening the instructional and disciplinary content of junior school education in favour of play activities. The man from the Ministry based his case on a thinly veiled philosophy of Naturalism with its roots in Rousseau. I pointed out to him that, whatever might be the practical merits or demerits of the new emphasis suggested for training junior school teachers, it could not go forward in a Church college under the impetus of the particular philosophy his case had rested upon. This, I argued, was not a question of his opinion or my opinion. Among the very minimum propositions that a Church college was by its very nature committed to, was the doctrine of Original Sin which his philosophy belied.

My contribution to the discussion was held to be a joke in rather bad taste. In trying to bring Christian thinking to bear upon an educational issue in a Church college, I discovered that I had entered a field of discourse reserved for eccentrics. Now I do not mind being disagreed with. I even relish it. But I find it depressing to be the sole inhabitant of a field of discourse which seems to me to be, not only a healthy one, but in fact the only right and proper one for discussion of the particular subject in the particular context. Were it appropriate to do so, one could fill a book with lamentations over the failure of the Church training colleges to resist the powerful secularizing pressures playing upon them as institutions which ought to be thinking christianly about the aims and process of education and about the human creatures it touches.

The standardizing influence of the Ministry of Education has weighed heavily on these colleges, and their development illustrates what it means to secularize a community, not by officially denying its religion, but by so departmentalizing it that it is deprived of any overt influence upon the community's conscious purpose and activities. Christianity is emasculated of its intellectual relevance. It remains a vehicle of spirituality and moral guidance at the individual level perhaps; at the communal level it is little more than an expression of sentimentalized togetherness.

The mental secularization of Christians means that nowadays we meet only as worshipping beings and as moral beings, not as thinking beings. We agree that it is right to be present on the Lord's own day in the Lord's own house. We agree that it is sinful to commit adultery or to slander our neighbours. But we cannot meet, as thinking Christians, over the controversial political, social, and cultural issues whose airing constitutes the vigorous intellectual life of many both inside and outside the Church. This is not because there are no propositions on which we can agree with fellow-Christians, but because there is no common field of discourse in which we can dispute either harmoniously or inharmoniously, unless we step first out of our theological skins. One knows Christian acquaintances with whom one cannot broach any political topic because they cannot allow that any argument is open upon which the *Daily Telegraph* has already pronounced. One knows Christian acquaintances with whom one cannot broach any educational topic because they cannot conceive that any policy or practice could be open to question which has the backing of the secular Establishment. The reader may think that these points

16

merely illustrate people's ignorance and their lack of capacity for independent thought. But there is another issue entangled with the issue of people's ignorance and imitativeness. I mean the lack of any used field of discourse for people thinking christianly about either politics or culture, and the consequent inability of people to step outside the recognized secular frames of reference established to contain political thinking and cultural thinking. In the modern world, by the very nature of our civilization, one cannot expect large numbers of people to be capable of truly independent thought. All the more reason why one must lament the lack of any tradition of discourse *for people to be dependent upon* in, say, political discussion, except the conformist tradition of specifically political politics. If only there were an inhabited field of discourse where Christians were thinking christianly about everything, there would be something nutritive for Christian minds to feed on. But Christian personalities are being truncated and deformed by the fact that men and women have to leap about from one tradition of discourse to another as they move in thought and discussion from moral matters to political matters, from ecclesiastical matters to cultural matters.

At this point the cynic might argue that we are well rid of Christian thinking from the political field. He might claim that thinking christianly about politics has been in the past productive of more bitterness, strife, and bloodshed than has thinking politically about politics. He might point to, say, the bloody struggle between the Covenanters and the government in seventeenth-century Scotland as evidence of what thinking christianly about politics does to the common weal. Certainly we have to admit that the stability and

17

comparative harmony of our government and our political life in this country have been achieved partly by excluding from a large area of political life the discussion of fundamental principles—the kind of principles which men regard as too sacred to be compromised, the kind on which they are ready to stake their well-being and their lives.

In short we have, both at the public level and at the private level, a positively nurtured negative attitude towards ideas, ideals, and theories. In so far as we are admired as a nation for the health of our political life and for our freedom from civil dissension and upheaval, it is largely due to that British pragmatism which brushes aside theoretical issues that might arouse furious controversy, and gets on with the immediate job in hand. The English philosophy in this respect is a simple one. If six people disagree violently about where they want to go, the best thing to do is to set them to work making a car so that, in the long run, they *can* go *somewhere*, easily and comfortably. Meantime one hopes that something external may occur which will provide an obvious reason for going to one destination rather than another. Or indeed the finished car might, by a lucky fluke, turn out to have a convenient if unforeseen technical bias in its steering which inclines it to turn in one direction rather than another. And until the hour of decision arrives, there is a tacit understanding among the six makers of the car that all reference to its future use will be rigidly excluded from their conversation. They will do their best to compensate for any frustrations on this score by talking fast and furiously about the mechanics of manufacture and the relative merits of various petrols, lubricants, plugs, and batteries. This arrangement once accepted, the fellow who persists

18

in raising awkward questions like—Where are we going to go? or, What is the point of making a car anyway? and, Why not make a washing-machine instead?—this fellow is regarded with contempt by his companions as being ill-bred, fatuously literal, absurdly doctrinaire, totally unpractical, and in the last resort a bore. He merits, in the upshot, the ultimate condemnation of the British mind. He can't get on with people.

Idealists are the most tortured people in our midst. We get along very nicely with cranks and foreigners. We are tolerant of rogues and criminals. But idealists—those people who insist on logically relating principle to practice, end to means, purpose to process, goal to route—we have no time for them. Literally no time. There is too much to do. Their misgivings would slow us up, prevent us even from making a start. Besides they would set us all at each other's throats in fierce controversy if once they were allowed a sober hearing. The best thing is to shut them up.

Publicly and privately, this has been a cardinal axiom of British life. In many circles it is bad form to introduce a serious proposition into conversation. Hence the establishment of the Sherry Party as the staple means of sociability in certain classes. The nature of a Sherry Party is such that serious conversation is impossible. A sustained triviality and flippancy are demanded by the very mechanics of the Sherry Party. A dinner party at which, after a meal, an intimate circle is formed round the fire is, by contrast, a dangerous and inflammatory mode of sociability. It is likely to produce reflective conversation into which earnestly held convictions may intrude. Such expressions of conviction are held to be damaging to the harmony of private life as to the harmony of public life.

One may justly say that our Public School tradition has actively encouraged an attitude to life which makes a strong distinction between the theoretical and the practical, and which gives to ideas and ideals the status of leisure-time interests not to be taken too seriously and on no account to be related to practical affairs. Tom Driberg, in his book on Guy Burgess, quotes a revealing letter by Robert Birley (later Headmaster of Eton). Birley is in this letter recommending Guy Burgess to his new Housemaster, a Mr Dobbs.

> It is refreshing to find one who is really well-read and who can become enthusiastic or have something to say about most things from Vermeer to Meredith. He is also a lively and amusing person. . .

We have here in a nutshell perhaps the definition of one "type" which the English Public Schools have set out to produce: one who can "become enthusiastic or have something to say about most things from Vermeer to Meredith". The essential triviality of this ideal is noteworthy. Does it matter whether one is becoming enthusiastic over what is important or over what is petty? Does it matter whether what one has to say about most things represents a balanced, sound, wise judgement? Or is the crucial thing that one should be lively and amusing?

Many things are wrong with the human ideal roughly hinted at here. In the first place genuine value-judgements are discounted. Enthusiasm, volubility, liveliness, and amusingness are the desired qualities. And none of these is related to an objective value. Hitler was enthusiastic. He also had something to say about most things. So what? Are we not concerned with what people are enthusiastic about, with the truth or falsity of what they say about most things? Is there no value in having nothing to say about many things? Does it not matter a good deal whether what one is being amusing about is the kind of issue which ought to form the basis for frivolity or wit? Questions bristle around Birley's commendation, which is one of the neatest of those little off-the-cuff pieces of accidental self-revelation that the Public School system continually throws to us. The irony of it all is touchingly pressed home in Burgess's subsequent career.

One of the reasons why we have no tradition of Christian thinking about contemporary affairs is that we have been thus taught to view with disfavour any earnest attachment to ideas and ideals such as would bring the heat of theoretical controversy into the arena of practical life. There is no doubt that we have reaped advantages from this attitude in our national life. But we have paid the price in the decay and now almost total disappearance of the Christian mind. For the Christian mind cannot exist *in vacuo*. It can exist only as fruitfully influencing action and being fed or disciplined in turn by the responsive logic of events. It is no accident that in a country in which there is no Christian political party there is also in many polite and influential circles a refusal to regard earnest conversation, which treats grave matters gravely, as a fit occupation for human beings except within the walls of a classroom.

One of the results of this attitude is that (except when passing judgement upon Russia) we have emptied political action of moral content. Let me quote the *Observer* for Sunday 9 July 1961, commenting upon Sir Anthony Eden's acceptance of an earldom:

> As Prime Minister, Sir Anthony Eden committed a great and multiple error of political judgment whose magnitude has become only more clear in the five years since he left office as a sick man.

21

This of course refers to the Suez venture. At the time the *Observer* was implacably hostile to the invasion by British troops. Every Christian had the duty to consider carefully whether the Suez aggression was a good act or an evil act. It seemed to me understandable at the time that Christians like Trevor Huddleston should pronounce upon it immediately as an evil act. Those who were genuinely convinced that it was a good act had always an equal right to be heard. From the vehemence of the *Observer's* attack upon Eden in 1956 it was plain that the *Observer* itself took a moral view. Now we have the act summed up as a "great and multiple error of political judgment". This is not the language of Christendom. Let men believe that the invasion of Egypt was a good act: let them believe it was an evil act. Let them take their stand accordingly. But to call the invasion a mistake is to lift the whole business of vital international action out of the sphere of the truly human activity upon which truly human judgements can be passed. Man is a moral being. His actions are good or evil. And it *matters* whether they are good or evil. In the case of decisions committing thousands of human beings to bloodshed, it matters enormously whether they are good or evil.

But no. On our side, this side the Iron Curtain, there are no evil decisions or actions. There are only mistakes. Evil is something which attaches to the decisions and actions of Soviet politicians. We refuse to dissociate ourselves from the Portuguese government for its repressive measures in Angola. We prevent the United Nations observers from entering South-West Africa in order to fulfil their internationally imposed obligations. It is as a Christian that decisions like these offend me. Suppose that, as a Christian, I accordingly take up

22

my pen to protest to my Member of Parliament. Should I get from my Member of Parliament the reply of a Christian to a Christian? The very question constitutes a joke. Most of our M.P.s would probably call themselves Christians. Do you think there are six M.P.s in the whole country, do you think there is one, who in reply to a Christian's protest would reply as a Christian and not as the slave of a party machine? Yet we prate of our independence and our freedom.

Having emptied political life of moral content, we have as a nation been unwilling to accept the consequences. If prophets tell us that our public life has been reduced to bare expediency stripped of altruism and idealism, we call them cynics. We cannot endure to face cleanly and honestly what we have done in obliterating the moral criterion and the spiritual dimension from our manipulation of people in the spheres of political, public, and institutional life. We have therefore invented a pseudo-value which will throw over decisions and actions that are purely expedient and pragmatic an air of respectability. I mean the alleged virtue of loyalty, which is useful to give a bogus moral quality to a slavish acceptance of the party line.

It might be argued that the problem of loyalty is the key problem of our age—in this country at least. Bertrand Russell is reputed to have said in a broadcast, "Loyalty is always evil". It is an exaggeration, of course; but it makes a profound point provocatively and, like so many of Russell's judgements, does more for the stimulation of healthy thinking than a thousand pulpit platitudes.

Loyalty may be said to be evil in the sense that if any action is defended on the grounds of loyalty alone, it is defended on no rational grounds at all. "I do this out of loyalty to my party" is irrational and amoral unless it is consequent upon, "My party is operating wholly and in every particular for the benefit of the human race". "I do this out of loyalty to my leader" is irrational and amoral unless it is consequent upon, "My leader's character, or purpose, or policy, is such that it ought to be supported". Loyalty is in itself not a moral basis for action. Loyalty to a good man, a good government, a good cause, is of course a different matter. But in these cases, where one stands by a man, or a government, or a cause, because it is good, one is standing by the good. The basis of action in these cases is moral in that one is serving the good; and thus the concept of loyalty is redundant. One can therefore say fairly that whenever the virtue of loyalty is quoted as a prime motive or basis for action, one has the strongest reasons for suspecting that support is being sought for a bad cause. There is no need to drag in the pseudo-virtue of loyalty if genuine values are being served in the course that is recommended. In this sense it may be said that loyalty is a sham virtue exploited to give a bogus moral flavour to amoral or immoral actions. We breathe the word "loyalty" and immediately a sentimental warmth floods our minds. We get the emotional kick which properly accompanies decisions made in the interest of noble causes. Our complacency is cheaply earned. We have evaded the necessity to scrutinize policies with our best Christian judgement; we have acted in the way calculated to keep us in with the powers-that-be; we have followed the herd. We have done all this and at the same time acquired a cosy feeling in the stomach of virtuous achievement. Loyalty is a key concept in modern life; and it does enormous damage to our moral fibre.

It follows from this that our political life in this country is riddled with moral self-deception. It may be still possible for a good Christian to be a good politician. There are inspiring examples which suggest that it is. But it is probably quite impossible for a good Christian to be a highly successful politician. There are some notable examples of frustrated careers that would support this view.

But of course it is not only in political life that we set aside individual Christian judgement in the interests of keeping the machinery ticking over. This attitude is a feature of life in all our institutions, commercial, cultural, and social. Certainly it is a feature of life in all the educational institutions I have experienced, whether they have been officially Christian or not. From day to day one is occupied in keeping the machinery of an institution going whilst, as a Christian, rejecting at a profound level the policy and principles professedly served by those who give the machine its direction. I mean that if you work in the English educational system you are to some extent inevitably furthering the policy of the Ministry of Education though you may well be at loggerheads with it. As a thinking Christian you will necessarily be at loggerheads with it because it is a pragmatically conceived policy, heavily secularist in its dominant motives. This sort of situation is, I take it, characteristic of the intelligent man's dilemma in the modern world.

We are all caught up, entangled, in the lumbering day-to-day operations of a machinery working in many respects in the service of ends which, as Christians, we reject. There is no way out other than suicide on the one hand or the acceptance of a specifically Religious vocation on the other. And this situation, the present

25

personal situation of thousands of thinking Christians, is the end product of a process that began the day Christians first decided to stop thinking christianly in the interests of national harmony, the day when Christians first felt that the only way out of endless public discussion was to limit the operation of acute Christian awareness to the spheres of personal morality and spirituality. From that point the spheres of political, cultural, social, and commercial life became dominated by pragmatic and utilitarian thinking. The Christian has believed—and still tries to believe—that he can enter these spheres of activity without yielding anything to the World, that he can enter trailing clouds of spirituality which will magically transform the atmosphere around him, that he can enter without accepting the pragmatic mode of discourse dominating thought and decision in these fields. He has erred. It cannot be done. As a Christian you may enter these spheres determined to be the leaven. But your leavening influence is restricted to the narrow field of personal relations and moral attitudes. You cannot enter these spheres as a *thinking* Christian, for there is no one to communicate with christianly. There is no field of discourse in which your presuppositions can be understood, let alone accepted or discussed. Within these fields you will find yourself inevitably, by acquiescence, subscribing to the furtherance of aims of which you deeply and christianly disapprove.

For this reason it may be said that Eichmann is the type of twentieth-century man. His trial seems to me to sum up and symbolize the guilt of twentieth-century man. It is a trial in which we are all implicated, as we were never implicated in the trials of Goering or Ribbentrop. Eichmann's guilt is our guilt in a sense in which neither Hitler's nor Himmler's guilt touched us. Eichmann is the archetype of our age, the supreme Organization Man. He kept the system going. He did his best to smooth the day-to-day operation of the system in which he found himself. The position he had reached was reached through the exercise and fulfilment of natural ambition within the social set-up he was educated to. He was *loyal*. The fundamental principles at the bottom of the system he served were not his responsibility. The aim and direction of that system's day-to-day operations it was not his business to question. There was a job to do. His fellow-countrymen, his friends and relations, were suffering and dying in dutiful obedience to the very same system his own activities furthered and served. He was loyal. May God even yet deliver us from the sin of loyalty.

We twentieth-century Christians have chosen the way of compromise. We withdraw our Christian consciousness from the fields of public, commercial, and social life. When we enter these fields we are compelled to accept for purposes of discussion the secular frame of reference established there. We have no alternative — except that of silence. We have to use the only language spoken in these areas. Our own Christian language is no longer understood of the people there. Moreover we ourselves have so long ceased to use it except for discussion of the moral, the liturgical, or the spiritual, that it is rusty and out of date. We have no Christian vocabulary to match the complexities of contemporary political, social, and industrial life. How should we have? A language is nurtured on usage, not on silence, however high-principled. And we have long since ceased to bring Christian judgement to bear upon the secular public world.

27

The Church's virtual withdrawal from these fields has left the pragmatists and utilitarians in power. It has led to the decay of the Christian mind. And now, by reaction, it has begotten a brood of frustrated Christians who try to cultivate their own souls but, outside of that, just don't know what to do. I suppose it was to answer this frustration that a group of young men a few years ago started the new Anglican monthly journal, *Prism.*

If we turn to the sphere of strictly personal morality, as opposed to the spheres of public and institutional life, we find a different story. There is, for instance, a full and lively Christian dialogue now being carried on in our midst on the subject of divorce and remarriage. This does not mean that there is a single healthy Christian attitude to this matter, reflecting a Christian mind wholly uncorrupted by secularist thinking. Far from it. But at least the public is made aware of divorce as a matter which has driven a wedge between Christian and secularist notions of human well-being and human duty. The subject is talked about, it is aired in the Press, it is tussled with sometimes in romantic fiction such as Waugh's *Brideshead Revisited.*

But there is no comparable Christian dialogue about, say, advertising, though it is surely a comparable source of evil in the modern world. Here is a topic which arouses the passion of many non-Christian rebels. No thinking man can consider the force and use of advertising in the modern world without being gravely disturbed. If he is a Christian, he will be disturbed *qua* Christian. Yet there is no field of discourse in which advertising is treated christianly. Nevertheless it is a live and important issue. Modern mass media are forming not only mentalities but total personalities on a vast

28

scale. It is not just that we are being seduced by advertisers to buy X's chocolate instead of Y's. We, or our
fellow-men, are being conditioned by advertisers to
believe that such and such things constitute the fullness
of life. An ideal of the full life is being hammered daily
into the minds of our fellow-men—even our young,
impressionable children. This ideal is cynically materialistic. We are being taught to treat worldly possessions as
status symbols rather than as serviceable goods. In other
words we are being urged to possess things on the
grounds that we shall thus stand higher in the view of
our neighbours. In order to illustrate how far this process has gone, let me quote an advertisement taken, not
from the stuff put out by a commercial firm frankly
trying to push the sales of a detergent or a washing
machine, but by that most respected and respectable of
commercial institutions, a bank. I quote from the *Daily
Mail* of 3 July 1961:

> Just how do your neighbours rate *you*?
> Your neighbours rate you pretty highly? They consider you're
> well up-with-the-times? What makes you so sure? Is it because
> they see—
>> You driving your snappy bubble car?
>> You going into your bank?
>> Your washing machine being delivered?
>> Your T.V. aerial on the roof?
>
> If your neighbours *really* know what's what, they'll know you've
> "arrived" the day they see you going in and out of ——. The
> bank where so many people are opening accounts these days.
> Why? Because enterprising people like you, people who
> intend to make their mark in life, know this. A —— cheque book
> isn't just extremely useful, it's a visible sign that you're Some-
> body. If you haven't got that cheque book yet, drop in any day
> and have a word with your nearest —— manager. He'll be
> happy to tell you about the advantages of getting the full
> banking service —— give *all* customers.

29

The crudity of this appeal to vanity, snobbery, covetous-ness, is striking only because a bank is a newcomer to this field. For a long time we have accepted this kind of thing from manufacturers and marketers of goods. It exploits the human being's weaknesses. It builds an unworthy conception of life. It is destructive of true values and creative of false ones.

Suppose I myself were to ask a few questions. Namely, Are there Christians on this bank's Board of Directors? Are they ashamed of themselves? Are they going to do anything about it? If I were to ask these questions I should be considered to be hurling about meaningless provocations. I should be asked, first, to explain myself; to describe what possible connection there could be between having Christians on the Board of Directors and publishing or not publishing this advertisement. In other words, if I were to think and speak christianly about this advertisement, I should find myself treated as an eccentric lost in a private world of fantasy, a rambling incoherent fellow. It would not be long before the final condemnations would come, gentle at first ("A pity he's got such a chip on his shoulder. . . . Sour grapes, I suppose"), then gradually growing in force ("Lives in a world of his own"). Yet, to be honest, as a Christian I find this advertisement an evil thing. And by evil thing, I mean evil—not a great and multiple error of commercial judgement, but an evil thing. I mean that christianly. And I wish I knew personally a hundred Christians who would think about it in those terms. For if we began to think, there would be hope of eventual action. But no, the Christian mind does not feed the current dialogue about advertising.

Yet this is a feature of contemporary life that is weighing daily on the minds of those we are supposedly bringing up to live the Christian life. All around us are advertisements titivating sexual interests, tightening up covetous urges, tantalizing every appetite. And—it must be said now by the thinking Christian, for it is already being said by the thinking atheist—advertising, with all its subtle techniques of psychological conditioning and mass-suggestion, has now entered the political field. It is well known that at the last election the Conservative Party employed the services of an advertising firm. It is established that the image of the Prime Minister put across to the public was one doctored, if not designed, by professional publicists. In other words political leaders no longer prepare their election programme by asking themselves, What is it that I believe in? Instead they ask their paid publicists, What will sell me to the public?

Now if one talks like this about political leaders, one will be assumed to be talking politics. If one criticizes Tory leaders for employing P.R. men, one will be labelled left wing. If one criticizes Labour leaders for the same thing, one will be labelled right wing. To be offended as a Christian by the recourse of political leaders to the cheap and corrupting media of psychological conditioning is within one's rights as a free citizen, but it rouses no answering indignation from a thinking Christian public. One is sick of mere political attacks on this kind of abuse, motivated by political hostility and lust for power. One is sad to see ferocious hostility to this kind of abuse almost monopolized by men who care nothing for Christianity or any other religion. Yet there is no Christian mind touching on these grave matters, feeding a Christian opinion. And if the individual Christian chooses to touch upon them, he straightway, in the eyes of others, loses his status as a

31

Christian thinking christianly, and acquires the status of a secular radical blowing off his top.

Can a Christian conscientiously work in advertising? Ought a Christian to work in P.R.? Is it possible for a thinking Christian to accept the discipline of a party machine in the House of Commons?

These questions sound outrageous. Precisely. That is the point I wish to make. They *are* outrageous in the sense that they fit into no current category of speculation. There is no trodden field of discourse which can accommodate them. There is no mental frame of reference within which they can be weighed and pondered. There is no system of evaluation by which they can be analysed and judged. For men are not thinking christianly about either advertising or politics, to name only two spheres of contemporary activity. There is no Christian mind.

In this connection it is noteworthy how little Christian thinking enters into the current controversy about nuclear war. A great deal of recent discussion on the question whether the West ought to have recourse to nuclear weapons turns largely on the question whether war as war can any longer produce tolerable results. This of course is not even a moral question, still less a Christian one. For the question whether war is in itself a justifiable means to resort to is left out of account. It is as if a gang of thieves, long practised in successful though hazardous burglaries, were to argue whether stealing all the notes from all the banks in London, Birmingham, Liverpool, and Manchester, would be a supreme *coup* or a disastrous failure, in that the successful thieves would be left with material on their hands which would be useless in a subverted economy with no currency. In short would theft on this scale knock the

32

bottom out of thieving as a career, ruining it as a means of achieving satisfactory results? That is the kind of argument now being waged on the subject of nuclear war. Would such a war produce a situation in which war would have exploded itself as a means of achieving anything? Thus, in a paradoxical way, many of those who argue fervently against resort to nuclear war, and on behalf of the continued attention to conventional weapons, reveal unwittingly a deep worry lest war should now prove to be a useless tool. Behind much of the talk against nuclear war lies in fact a passionate and deeply ingrained attachment to war. Ironically, what worries many people is that the invention of nuclear weapons may have destroyed war. War, for them, has always been a kind of umbrella which you could put up at the last moment. Now a man who might have tried to dissuade our hypothetical thieves from raiding all the biggest banks in the country on the grounds that theft is evil, ought surely to be distinguished from one who tried to dissuade them on the grounds that, if they succeeded, they would kill thieving as a practical pursuit.

Again, Christian thinking seems to play only a very small part in the Campaign for Nuclear Disarmament. Study of their publicity suggests that the main C.N.D. platform is "Better Red than Dead". That is not a view which a Christian pacifist could subscribe to. The Christian cannot possibly accept death as the ultimate and final evil to be resisted at all costs. The Christian pacifist objects to killing, not to being killed. A Christian mind, working on the issues raised by C.N.D., would have to change the emphasis of the movement. Propaganda addressed to particular areas about what would happen to *your* town if an H-bomb were dropped on the nearest big city is not likely to search the Christian's conscience

33

deeply. For propaganda of this kind makes a crude appeal to our love of comfort, of the amenities of life, and of physical existence itself. In short it tries to play upon our basest fears. So far as the possibility of nuclear war is concerned, the Christian mind ought surely to be turned to such matters as the uncertainty whether radiation may not permanently, or at least for many generations, damage the human species, impairing numberless unborn children.

Attending to current controversies, as they are reflected in the Press, one is forced to the conclusion that the moral and often Christian pacifism of the 1920s and the 1930s has been replaced by a limited revulsion against nuclear weapons only. If this is so, I think there is a simple explanation. The First World War discredited war. But, in this country at least, the Second World War rehabilitated war. (This may turn out, in the long run, to have been the most tragic result of the Second World War.) The First World War, with its appalling casualty lists, with the plain senselessness of its carnage, was succeeded, not unnaturally, by a period in which the dominant cry was, "No more War". But the Second World War, with its appalling final revelations of the depths to which human nature had sunk under Nazism, was succeeded here, not unnaturally, by a period in which the dominant cry has been, "No more Totalitarianism".

Thus in the 1920s and 1930s it was a public speaker's assumed duty to round off his speech—whether it was at the laying of a foundation stone or the presentation of prizes at a school—with the theme "Never again". And this meant, no more war. Never again the trenches and the mud, and the heaped-up corpses, and the month after month of institutionalized barbarity. But in the

34

1950s and 1960s the public speaker's theme has been, not Never again war, but Never again tyranny and injustice, ghettoes and concentration camps, secret police and arrest in the night. And these were not so much aspects of war, as symptoms of the disease which the war had cured.

Many people brought up in the 1920s and 1930s had no clear idea what the First World War had achieved. The adjectives applied to it afterwards – *senseless*, *meaningless*, and the like – implied that it had not achieved anything. I cannot myself recall hearing, as a child, a single explanation of what the Allies had achieved in the First World War (except the defeat of Germany). Rather we were brought up to the conviction that nothing worth while had been achieved at all. But every child to-day knows what sort of a mess was cleaned up by the victory of the Allies in the Second World War. And of course the mess was cleaned up without, in this country, anything on the scale of the First War casualties.

The numberless war books and films reproducing the gallantries of the last war have been able, without falsity, to represent the thing as a struggle between men devoted to an evil cause and men devoted to a good one. The revelations of atrocities and torture committed by the Nazis have aroused a revulsion beside which the revulsion against military slaughter pales in comparison. These are some of the factors resulting in the rehabilitation of war, as a means to an end, by the events of 1939 to 1945. As the trial of Eichmann has recently reminded us, the Second World War removed evils which still outrage our moral sense more deeply than the evils of the war itself as generally presented to us.

I am not saying that there is no pacifist reply to this

35

claim. My purpose here and now is not to argue a thesis but to describe a situation. And the situation is one in which moral indignation has been switched from war itself as an evil to dictatorship as an evil; and of course an elaborate attempt has been made, in the U.S.A. especially, to transfer to Soviet Communism, lock, stock, and barrel, the whole burden of totalitarian guilt rightly borne by the Hitler régime.

It is no flippancy to say that an important aspect of our psychological dilemma in the West is this. That just when war has been for us emotionally justified up to the hilt, war is being taken from us as an unplayable game, an unusable tool. It is a grave and grotesque irony.

But we are in danger of being deflected into a digression by this subject which necessarily hangs at the back of our minds. The point really relevant to us here, in this context, is that there is no living Christian dialogue even on the subject of nuclear war. The nuclear war controversy which does exist is almost (not quite) wholly carried on within a secularist frame of reference. Whether this civilization of ours will continue to exist in its present form is the dominant concern.

After making this complaint about the lack of Christian thinking to-day, one will sometimes meet with the astonishing reply that there is no longer any need for Christian thinking. The argument is that, in the social and political spheres, though Christian thinking was very necessary in the days of injustice, poverty, and unemployment, it is quite unnecessary now that the Welfare State has been established to guarantee the social well-being of our fellow-citizens. It has been said that it would be a waste of effort for Christian thinkers

36

to devote their energies and attention to the field of social and political life in this country when the aims of Christian endeavour in this field have already been won.

Although the Christian must reject this argument as false and shallow, it is difficult for him not to feel a shred of secret sympathy with the mood which it represents. Each of us, when confronted with the apparently insuperable difficulty of thinking christianly about the British social and political set-up in the 1960s, is tempted to look back nostalgically to days when things were different. We recall the convenient confluence of religious and secular aims which gave Christians a clear social programme in the 1930s. There was the crying need to establish a just economy in the British Isles which would get rid of unemployment and eradicate the appalling distinctions between the very wealthy and the numerous poor. The major social evil of that period was readily recognizable—injustice and in-equality. Looking back to our youth, we recall the emotional stirrings, the deep sense of Christian purposiveness, when a Temple, say, challenged the existing social order in the name of Christ; and in the name of our Lord put the Church in this land at the side of those working against privilege and vested interests towards a new deal for the poor. But what now? Where is our Christian duty, our Christian aim, our Christian programme, within the shelter of the Welfare State? We do not know: we cannot say. Yet our ignor-ance and silence are not, certainly not, due to the fact that the Welfare State has made Christian thinking out of date and irrelevant. The reason we have nothing to say to the contemporary situation is that we have not been thinking about the contemporary situation. We stopped thinking about these things years ago. We stopped thinking christianly outside the scope of personal morals and personal spirituality. We got into the habit of stepping out of our Christian garments whenever we stepped mentally into the field of social and political life. Because the subject was social or political, we left all our well-tried and well-grounded Christian concepts behind us, and adopted the vocabulary of secularism. We put aside talk of vocation, or God's Providence, or man's spiritual destiny, and instead chattered with the rest about productivity, assembly-line psychology, and deployment of personnel. Most ironical of all, we thought we were really being down-to-earth practical Christians when we went in for this kind of thing. We threw off our theology, dived into the factories, and solemnly announced that at last we were bringing the Church to the people.

Whenever one tries to make a point of this kind, forcefully and concretely, one is in danger of appearing to discredit worthy work by devoted Christians. That is the last thing intended here. I am fully aware of what has been positively achieved by such bodies as the Industrial Christian Fellowship, and this must not be construed as an attack upon either their work or their attitudes. (I say this because I have been misunderstood on a similar topic before.) But the fact remains that the psychological sequence I have described—caricatured, if you like—has been a powerful and misleading feature in our Christian life during the last fifteen years. We have too readily equated getting into the world with getting out of our theology. The result has been that we have stopped thinking christianly. We have *behaved* christianly, some of us; in cases even heroically and self-sacrificingly. We have prayed and worshipped christianly. Then we have gone back to talk politics with the politician, social welfare with the social worker, labour relations with the trade unionist, and we have emptied our brains of Christian vocabulary, Christian concepts, in advance, just to make sure that we should get fully into touch. Thus we have stepped mentally into secularism. We have trained, even disciplined ourselves, to think secularly about secular things and—irony of ironies—have even managed to persuade ourselves that there was something more Christian about giving way in this matter and accepting the other fellow's mental environment. In this way the Christian mind has died of neglect and disuse. If you begin a sentence with the word "God" you are assumed to be preaching, and propriety requires that you reserve utterances of that kind for the pulpit. We have brought this situation upon ourselves by encouraging the world in the belief that the secular mind is the proper instrument for weighing, analysing, and evaluating the secular world.

An important contributory factor to the loss of mental morale by the Church has been a misguided conception of Christian charity. It has been assumed that the charitable man suppresses his views in the same way that he subordinates personal interest. A wild fantasy has taken hold of many Christians. They have come to imagine that just as the unselfish man restrains himself from snatching another piece of cake, so too he restrains himself from putting forward his point of view. And just as it is bad form to boast about your private possessions or loudly recapitulate your personal achievements, so too it is bad form to announce what your convictions are. By analogy with that charity of the spirit which never asks or claims but always gives and gives again, we have manufactured a false "charity" of the mind, which never takes a stand, but continually yields ground. It is proper to give way to other people's interests: therefore it is proper to give way to other people's ideas.

The damage done by this false deduction has been enormous. It is urgently necessary to clear the air on this matter. A man's religious convictions and understanding of the truth are not private possessions in the sense that his suit and the contents of his note-case are private possessions. It is worthy, no doubt, when you have been asked for your overcoat, to give away your jacket as well. But it is no exercise in Christian charity, when you have been requested in argument to drop your absurd belief in the apostolic succession, to offer to surrender your belief in the sacraments too. Your beliefs, as a Christian, are not yours in the sense that you have rights over them, either to tamper with them or to throw them away. Of course the very fact that nowadays we look upon convictions as personal possessions is a symptom of the disappearance of the Christian mind. It is precisely in such odd and scarcely graspable notions that the full extent of the secularization of the modern mind is glimpsed. One of the crucial tasks in reconstituting the Christian mind will be to re-establish the status of objective truth as distinct from personal opinions; to rehabilitate knowledge and wisdom in contradistinction from predilection and whim. That topic, however, belongs to a later chapter in this book.

The sphere of the intellectual, the sphere of knowledge and understanding, is not a sphere in which the Christian gives ground, or even tolerates vagueness and confusion. There is no charity without clarity and firmness.

Having now, in a variety of ways, illustrated my thesis that there is no longer a Christian mind, I ought perhaps

40

to defend myself in advance against the direct contradiction. I have argued that we are not thinking christianly about politics, social affairs, industry, culture, education, or indeed any of the vital fields of human activity generally regarded as the domain of secularism. In reply, a critic might point to a book here which examines capitalist society in the light of Christian doctrine, and a book there which studies the application of Christian principles in the industrial field. The critic might cite writers who have individually striven to bridge the gap between the Christian religion and the field of economics, or between the Christian religion and the study of sociology. My claim that we are not thinking christianly about secular activities is not invalidated by pointing to a few books by a few individuals. Indeed I have written a book myself on the relationship between the Christian Faith and the drift of educational and cultural thinking, and I nevertheless assert that we are not thinking christianly about education or culture. Such efforts as have been made to remedy this deficiency have been scattered and, comparatively speaking, little noticed. It cannot be said that any of these efforts has yet created a field of discourse. And in any case a good deal of what has been written in the attempt to bridge the gaps comes into the category of what I should call secular thinking trimmed with pious platitudes. There is small wonder that this is the case. The Christian mind has been so enfeebled by disuse that those who strive now to put it into working order again feel like pioneers in a strange and virgin country. The language of the local inhabitants lacks vocabulary to fit the notions the pioneers would wish to introduce. The minds of the local inhabitants are unequipped to receive the concepts the visitors are anxious to establish. To many who set out with high ideals and rigorous intentions, it seems better to talk with the natives in their own tongue about the things they do understand, in the hope that sooner or later, here or there, one may be enabled by good fortune to sneak in a few comments hinting at the enormous message one set out to convey.

Before proceeding further, I ought perhaps to issue a caveat. By the nature of my thesis I have necessarily kept repeating, in this chapter, that Christian thought has not been adequately at work on a variety of topics. As such topics are surveyed, the reader is likely to be provoked to the question, What are you getting at? What line do you want the Christian to take on this or that issue? It is not within the scope of this book to answer questions in that way. Indeed the basic argument of this book is that these subjects have not been thought about christianly. And since they have not yet been thought about christianly, it follows that we are obviously not in a position to proclaim a lot of Christian answers to the problems of the day. By the nature of the situation, answers are a long way off.

Does this mean that here is one more book that stirs up a problem and then just leaves it, well and truly stirred? Is there no positive thesis to match our disturbing charge that the Church's intellectual morale has reached a low ebb?

There is, I hope, a very positive side to my case. We cannot say here and now what the Christian line should be on this or that secular problem. We are not immediately seeking a "Christian line". There is something before the achievement of a Christian line — and that is a Christian dialogue in which a given issue can be explored and known by the thinking Church. And even that is not the beginning. For there is something before the Christian dialogue, and that is the Christian mind—a mind trained, informed, equipped to handle data of secular controversy within a framework of reference which is constructed of Christian presuppositions. The Christian mind is the prerequisite of Christian thinking. And Christian thinking is the prerequisite of Christian action. That is why I have chosen to write about the Christian mind. Because two streams of experience in my life—that of study and that of practical day-to-day contact with fellow-Christians—have converged to convince me that under all the frustrations of inactivity from which Churchmen suffer, under all the misuse of energy, mental and manual, which the Church delights in, and under the appalling catastrophe of a world cut off from the Church, there lies a deficiency, a gaping hole, where there ought to be the very bedrock basis of fruitful action, the Christian mind.

2

THINKING CHRISTIANLY AND
THINKING SECULARLY

HAVING POSITED a Christian mind, it is our
duty to define it so as to distinguish it clearly
from the secular mind. When we have defined
the Christian mind—in terms of the religious view of
life which is its constant frame of reference—we shall
be in a position to distinguish more exactly between the
process of thinking christianly and that of thinking
secularly. One prevalent confusion of thought must be
swept aside in advance, however, and that is the confusion which would equate thinking christianly with
thinking about Christian matters.

To think secularly is to think within a frame of reference bounded by the limits of our life on earth: it is to
keep one's calculations rooted in this-worldly criteria.
To think christianly is to accept all things with the mind
as related, directly or indirectly, to man's eternal destiny
as the redeemed and chosen child of God.

You can think christianly or you can think secularly
about the most sacred things—the sacrament of the
altar, for example. Likewise you can think christianly or
you can think secularly about the most mundane
things—say, about a petrol pump. You would have to
think secularly about the sacrament of the altar if you
were required to budget financially for a year's supply
of wine and wafers for your parish church. At the other

44

extreme, to think christianly about a petrol pump would be to ponder the place of petrol and of motor vehicles generally in the ethos and practice of a Christian society in a God-given world. No doubt, if exhaustively pursued, the issue would raise such questions as — How far is the widespread use of motor vehicles increasing the slavery of men to machinery and consequently impairing man's delicately balanced status as a spiritual being in a material world? Are the inventions of modern technology being used for the betterment of human life over our planet as a whole, or are they being used as stimulants to covetousness and self-indulgence in the lives of a selfish minority of the world's inhabitants? Is the increasingly mechanical nature of contemporary civilization dragging man away, not only from his natural roots in mother earth, but also from his supernatural roots in the divine order?

There is nothing in our experience, however trivial, worldly, or even evil, which cannot be thought about christianly. There is likewise nothing in our experience, however sacred, which cannot be thought about secularly — considered, that is to say, simply in its relationship to the passing existence of bodies and psyches in a time-locked universe. Thus, paradoxically, at a time when there is a great ferment of thought about religious matters, about the Church, the Bible, the Christian past and the Christian future, there might be a steadily diminishing stream of strictly Christian thinking. One might argue that such is indeed our situation to-day. Perhaps never was there more secular thinking about things Christian.

The fields of discourse to which this applies are numerous. Write a study of the Church in the reign of Queen Anne or a History of the Oxford Movement, and you will find yourself in a vital field of discourse. It is of course an important field of discourse too: here is no attempt to belittle it. Nevertheless it can be characterized as an essentially secular field of discourse in so far as the data are analysed, elucidated, shaped, and commented upon by a mind operating within exactly the same frame of reference as would be adopted by, say, an atheistic historian of the Russian Revolution or the Court of Louis XIV.

The fact that many people are writing about things Christian is in itself irrelevant to the question whether there is still a Christian mind. So too is the fact that many people are thinking and talking about Christian issues. For you might write a book about, say, the ecumenical movement, without once lapsing into specifically Christian thinking. You might tussle with the practical problem of trying to unite Christian bodies each with its own system of government. You might survey the theoretical issues raised by trying to bring into mutual relationship Christian bodies each with its own doctrinal emphases. You might dwell at length on the great advantages to be gained from unity and the high cost of continuing disunity in terms of moral authority and influence. You might do all this, and much more, and yet never stray outside the same framework of political and social principles and notions which would be brought into play in a book dealing with the advantages and disadvantages of a nationalized railway system as opposed to a network of regional companies under private ownership. Or, to take another example, it is perfectly possible, it is even natural, to write a book on the subject of Church unity whose recommendations would explore the modes of political negotiation and manoeuvre proper to the working out

46

of such problems as that of the entry of Britain into the European Common Market.

The case of books on the ecumenical movement is cited, because in the sphere of ecumenicity a living dialogue is now being carried on. A well-trodden field of ecumenical discourse exists. And yet one may doubt whether, by and large, this represents a substantial body of Christian thinking. Some of it seems to subsume even the most sacred matters under secularly conceived categories. Questions of episcopacy, apostolic authority, the sacramental system, the priestly office, and so on, are handled within secular frames of reference as used for the manipulation of rival claims in the industrial or political world. Much of the thinking tends to be this-worldly. It is directed towards fashioning an institution homogeneous and efficient after the pattern of commercial and political organizations. Sometimes it is dominated by procedures of bargain and compromise more proper to the market or the embassy than to the Church. Contributors to the discourse balance point against point, staking this and risking that, winning here and losing there, as one might on the casino or the Stock Exchange. There is thrust, manoeuvre, parry, withdrawal, and all the contrivances of political summitry.

Here, however, we must insert another warning against possible misunderstanding. It is not part of our case to pretend that all secular thinking is bad and that all Christian thinking is good. We are not even saying that secular thinking about Christian matters is bad – or even inappropriate. It is not. It is necessary. To think secularly may be to think well or ill, logically or illogically, illuminatingly or platitudinously, fruitfully or to no purpose. Likewise to think christianly may be to think well or ill, rationally or irrationally, knowledgeably or ignorantly, penetratingly or shallowly, lucidly or confusingly. We are not wiping out any of the established categories and values pertinent to thought and to scholarship when we make this crucial distinction between thinking christianly and thinking secularly.

But having made that admission, we must face the facts of the present situation. Generally speaking, we are not thinking christianly except over a very narrow field. We are thinking secularly a great deal, even on Christian matters. That much of this secular thinking on Christian matters may be good and useful thinking in no way detracts from the urgency of the point stressed in this book. It desperately needs to be supplemented by more specifically Christian thinking.

Take a look at publishers' lists. Turn to the section headed Religion. You will find that by far the majority of the really sound and solid publications are instances of secular thinking about Christian matters. That is to say they are historical studies, textual commentaries on the meaning of documents, investigations into the authenticity of documents, surveys of the origin and growth of practices, biographies of the great figures of the past or of recent Churchmen whose claim on our attention is often less easy to establish, etymological studies of important words in the Christian vocabulary, surveys of organizational systems and techniques, factual accounts of Church activities in various parts of the world, and so on.

We are not saying that these studies are not important. Most of them may well be so. But they are often almost wholly constituted of secular thinking in the sense that they exemplify the secular mind recording, categorizing, evaluating, explaining, within the bounds of the same this-worldly frame of reference that the non-Christian

48

scholar employs in his studies of the secular world. This does not make them bad books or unnecessary books: but it does prevent them from being regarded as contributing to a specifically Christian dialogue, however good they may be. As evidence, therefore, of the continued existence or health of the Christian mind, they are nugatory.

It is not difficult to explain why, in England especially, high-quality Christian thinking about the secular world should be swamped by high-quality secular thinking about things Christian. We have believed that the main intellectual discipline of the future priest should be outside the theological field—history, literature, science, anything. We have allowed deeply secularist universities to establish in our future priests and bishops a thoroughly secular mind—*so far as the realm of the intellectual is concerned.* We have then tried to disinfect the mind of its secular orientation by one or two years of residence in a theological college where, of necessity, only a limited amount of time can be given to pure theological studies. Thus we have large numbers of priests and—truth compels us to admit—even bishops, who, whilst they are versed in the right things to say about personal morality and the spiritual life, are not practised in thinking christianly beyond those limits. When they broach any subject of immediate secular concern in the political or social field, they tend to fall back upon pious platitudes. They are past-masters at fence-sitting. Indeed many of them, devoted as they are to liberal notions of broad-mindedness and toleration, have rationalized their ignorance into the comforting conviction that fence-sitting is pre-eminently the posture of the charitable Christian leader.

Similarly our bishops and clergy, starved as they often

49

are of theology, bring acute but secular thinking to bear upon Christian matters. The scholars among them, professors and bishops and deans, produce numerous books revealing great knowledge of history and languages. This output would be an occasion for great rejoicing were it only balanced by a comparable output of books reflecting christianly on the world we live in. But the voice of prophecy is silent.

Of course, the Church apart, it is a feature of our culture generally that as we are rich in scholars so we are poor in thinkers. Occasionally, very occasionally, a man may be both a first-rate scholar and a first-rate thinker. But the nature of our modern educational system is such that this happy combination arises ever more rarely. Potential thinkers are being turned into mere scholars by the pressures of conformity so strong both in the educational world and in society at large. The thinker challenges current prejudices. He disturbs the complacent. He obstructs the busy pragmatists. He questions the very foundations of all about him, and in so doing throws doubt upon aims, motives, and purposes which those who are running affairs have neither time nor patience to investigate. The thinker is a nuisance. He is a luxury that modern society cannot afford. It will therefore naturally, and on its own terms justifiably, strive to keep him quiet, to restrict his influence, to ignore him. It will try to pretend that he does not exist.

Since the lot of the thinker in the secular world is so unattractive and frustrating, it is not surprising that we lack thinkers. But the Church cannot do without thinkers—or prophets, as she is wont somewhat pompously to call them. She cannot afford to ape the secular world in suppressing the thinker, in trying to replace him by the scholar. She destroys herself in doing so.

For the secular world is true to itself in rejecting the thinker. It serves the laws of its own preservation in rejecting him. But the Church is false to itself when it rejects the thinker. And therefore, in so far as it adopts the fashion of the secular world and tries to submerge thought under learning, prophecy under scholarship, wisdom under know-how, it strives to secularize itself; in other words to destroy itself.

The scholar and the thinker are in some ways mutually antithetical types. Scholarship cannot endure exaggeration. Thinking cannot thrive without it. There is no thinking without exaggeration. As Ortega y Gasset puts it—

> To think is, whether you want or no, to exaggerate. If you prefer not to exaggerate, you must remain silent; or, rather, you must paralyse your intellect and find some way of becoming an idiot.

(The reader will note that I am more indulgent than Gasset in that I allow the scholar as well as the idiot to eschew exaggeration.) The scholar evades decisiveness; he hesitates to praise or condemn; he balances conclusion against competing conclusion so as to cancel out conclusiveness; he is tentative, sceptical, uncommitted. The thinker hates indecision and confusion; he firmly distinguishes right from wrong, good from evil; he is at home in a world of clearly demarcated categories and proven conclusions; he is dogmatic and committed; he works towards decisive action.

To typify the extremes in this way is useful, but must not be taken too literally. For the scholar, as thus characterized, is not the only man who studies: and the thinker, as thus characterized, is not the only man who thinks. Obviously there is no scholar who does not think; and there is no thinker who is quite devoid of scholarship. Nevertheless the distinction between

51

Scholarship and Thinking is a fruitful one to ponder: and at least it will serve to indicate that just as there is a dearth of Christian thinking in the Church, so in our secular culture there is a dearth of pure thinking as opposed to that recording, commenting, and elucidating, which constitute scholarship. Thus our complaint against the education through which our priests and bishops are prepared for their duties might justly be widened into a complaint against the bias of our educational system in general. It is not geared to the production of thinkers. It is geared to their obliteration.

But we must not be deflected from our central thesis. Neither our bishops nor our clergy give us leadership in thinking christianly about the contemporary world. The inability of people to think christianly, even about Christian matters, has been vividly illustrated recently in the controversy over the English system of appointing bishops. Many of the arguments produced on either side have reflected a lamentable rash of secularist thinking, wholly this-worldly in its orientation. What a lot we could learn from the Orthodox Church in this respect. The Orthodox Church appoints its bishops only from among its monks. That is to say, it recognizes that the position of bishop has about it the accoutrements and status of worldly success. It therefore makes it impossible for a man to become a bishop unless he has first completely surrendered all his interest in self-advancement by taking vows of poverty, chastity, and obedience. Now I am not at the moment arguing that this would necessarily be the right machinery of election for our own Church. I *am* saying that only by thinking christianly about the appointment of bishops could men have arrived at the restrictions upon selection which the Eastern Church has imposed. An opponent of the Orthodox system might argue that it is bad because it could encourage men to take religious vows with selfish ulterior motives. To which one could reply: Bad or good, I'm not sure: but that the system stems from genuine attempts to think christianly and to act christianly, of that I am certain.

We might consider, by contrast, the kind of comments which have stood out in public discussion of episcopal appointments in our own country. And I would emphasize that, although controversy in England revolves around the peculiar system of appointing bishops in the Established Church, many of the mental attitudes reflected in that controversy are equally evident, for instance, in American discussion over the appointment of bishops in the Episcopal Church. Indeed, the basic question, whether we think christianly or secularly in choosing our bishops, is one that presses upon the whole Anglican Communion. The fact that it has recently been brought into prominence in the provinces of Canterbury and York by the creaking and rumbling of the ancient machinery of the Establishment is accidental to the main issue. We must therefore reflect upon the recent controversy in England over the system of appointing bishops with an eye on the deeper and more universal implications.

It has been argued that our system is good because it has worked well. To which one might reply that choosing bishops by taking names out of a hat might conceivably have worked very well indeed. But that would not make the random system of choice a good one. A system of election has to be, not only operationally effective, but also rationally justifiable. It has been argued that we have had the best men as bishops in the past. This seems to me a ghastly and almost blasphemous

53

libel on the heroic and saintly parish priests who have served the Church so well in the past, often frustrated by timorous shepherds whose prophetic zeal has been tamed to the level of garden-party votes of thanks and radio uplift. The best men? This succession of gaitered gentry who have sailed through the country's quadrangles, drawing-rooms, and clubs on that utterly unreal level of upper middle-class sociability, planting their genteel *bon-mots*, trimming their fastidious sails, lost to the world between the pages of *The Times*, Trollope, and the *Journal of Theological Studies*? The best men? Good men, yes no doubt, many of them; and anyway who are we to judge them—or anyone? But the best—in a Church which has produced those priests and religious whom you and I know as the great saints of the present? We all know one or two of them. We are not required to name or to praise them. But at least we should avoid the risk of insulting the faith they have heroically represented by pretending that those gaitered dignitaries who have constructed their own biographies on the public stage have been the best men we have.

To think christianly is to know in our souls that our bishops have not been the best men available, even taking into account the particular nature of the modern bishop's functions. The bishops, thinking christianly, ought surely to be the first to announce that they at least cannot defend the system of appointment on the grounds that it has effectively creamed off the élite of the Church's manpower. (The fact that there has been no episcopal outcry to this effect suggests indeed that the system of election has been much faultier than we thought it.) The Church as an institution is entangled in the weaknesses and deficiencies of human nature.

Its earthly set-up is necessarily corrupted by man's sinfulness and distorted by man's ignorance. But of course there is more to be said than that. For to think christianly is to accept the fact that in God's eyes it may be more important to have a thoroughly holy, wise, instructed man as parish priest in a slum area than to have such a man as bishop of the diocese. If there are not enough good men to go round, it may well be a part of the divine economy to make sure that the weakest ones go where they can do least damage — the episcopal bench, where their personal influence over the souls of the laity is reduced to a minimum, where the qualities of individual personality are of least significance. It may be quite unpractical, in God's eyes, to waste really good men in episcopal palaces. Surely, surely, to think christianly is to recognize that God may have answered our prayers for the Church by putting the least promising human material into episcopal thrones, where the authority of the higher office will strengthen them and guide them in their ignorance, and where the responsibilities of status will operate to restrain their natural foolishness.

I do not know. I am trying to think christianly. But perhaps the Devil has taken hold of my pen. If so, he has a better sense of humour than I have ever credited him with.

No doubt the high peak of secular thinking on this Christian problem was reached by the bishop who publicly claimed that it would be a bad thing to eradicate the element of mystery from the Christian religion, and that therefore the present system of appointing bishops behind a veil of secrecy was a good one. Here was an attempt to secularize a word soaked in religious significance, to empty it of Christian content and hand it

55

over to the godless for keeps. To speak of the mystery of the Christian religion is to use the vocabulary of the sanctuary. The mystery of holiness; the mystery of the Real Presence; the mystery of the Incarnation; the mystery of God's redeeming love. All these are rich and pertinent usages of the word *mystery* as connoting something proper to Christian faith and practice, as referring to the point at which man's understanding falters and his boldness fails before the shrouded and inconceivable ways of God. And this word was stripped of all its grandeur and wealth, to be used in defence of a huddle of civil servants and other top worldlings plotting the next episcopal promotion in a back-room off Whitehall!

It will be granted that the bishop's use of the word *mystery* was an instance of wholly secular thinking, the more dangerous because it masqueraded as Christian thinking, the more destructive because it tried to put real mysteries — some of the most sacred aspects of our religion — on the same level as the furtive secrecies of political manoeuvre. Indeed the bishop's verbal sleight of hand might be said to be on a par with the recommendation that since mystery is an essential ingredient of the Christian religion, therefore mystery novels ought to be compulsory reading in the choir stalls. Mystery, as a feature of Christianity, can never be equated with secrecy. Mystery has to do with the involuntary limitations of men before the nature and works of God. Secrecy has to do with conscious concealment.

There is of course no need to conceal the operations of a system which is good. The present English system of appointing bishops undoubtedly weakens the Church. A man may be convinced that it is a good system: but, if he is, his conviction is an irrational one since he is not in a position to prove or corroborate it. It is not enough for Churchmen to shake their head in pious disgust when the cynic says: "So-and-so was given his episcopal preferment because he ran to the support of the government when their attack upon Egypt came under ecclesiastical fire. So-and-so was given his episcopal preferment because he put in a good word for the H-bomb just when the nation's conscience was beginning to be disturbed by the thing. So-and-so has been careful to say the right things when trade unions have seemed to be getting out of hand. So-and-so, on the other hand, has been passed over again because he has been on the dangerous side in controversies like these." When charges of this kind are made, the Churchman must be able to refute them by pointing to the known machinery of promotion. We must be able to say, "It isn't a perfect system, but it's as just as we can make it." Even more urgent is the need for reform now that controversy has drawn so much open comment from the clergy. We must certainly forestall the situation in which a cynic could say: "So-and-so has got his reward for springing to the defence of the appointing system, while So-and-so has paid the price of attacking it."

The whole question, not only of the appointment of bishops, but also of the function of bishops, needs to be considered in relation to the basic theme of this book. (And more will be said about the matter later on.) The bishop's office is crucial, and if we allow our thinking about this office to be contained within a secular frame of reference, we shall do grave practical damage to the Church. It is a subject on which, oddly enough, the layman is peculiarly fitted to speak, because he is so obviously disinterested, and no one can turn upon him that diabolical refutation summed up in the phrase

"Sour grapes". Thus the layman is in a position to say the things which priests can only mutter in private. No man likes to make criticisms, however just, which evil-minded opponents might dismiss as the reflections of wounded self-interest. Many a strong case remains unexpressed because honest men will not give the supporters of the establishment the opportunity to pronounce them "disappointed men".

The bishop is a Father-in-God. In practice he has been turned into an Administrative Officer. Thus the appointment to bishoprics of men distinguished neither for their piety, their spirituality, nor their pastoral wisdom, is nowadays defended on the grounds that in the modern context a bishop must be a good administrator. One can scarcely think of a more thoroughly secular concept than that of the good administrator. One hesitates to go to the cynical length of asserting that "He's a good administrator" is a mere euphemism for "He's a thoroughly worldly man", but there is no doubt that administrative skill of the kind referred to is frequently little more than a slick know-how produced by a far too whole-hearted immersement in the most worldly aspect of worldly affairs. The administrative type, *par excellence*, as now bred in an increasingly mechanized and conformist society, is one who has learned to discount principle in favour of expediency, to subordinate ideals to utilitarian considerations, in short to be the pragmatist in action.

Nothing therefore could stand in more powerful contrast to the true Christian concept of the bishop than the current concept of the administrator. If we were to think christianly about the present situation, we should say: "This equation between episcopal and administrative function is intolerable, and indeed represents

CHRISTIAN AND SECULAR THINKING

the kind of worldly thinking which strikes at the roots of religion. It is necessary therefore to make the bishop once more a Father-in-God, by stripping from him his administrative function. A fit and proper beginning would be to nominate to bishoprics only men of known spiritual and pastoral gifts who will refuse to be turned into administrators. But instead of thinking christianly about this essentially Christian issue, we think secularly. We say: "In the present set-up the office of bishop has become an administrative office. Therefore we must appoint good administrators to bishoprics." In other words, instead of making the office of bishop the Christian thing it ought to be, we allow secular influences to secularize it. Since we refuse to think christianly even about the office of bishop, it is scarcely surprising that we lose the habit of thinking christianly about secular matters.

Of course my argument is to be distinguished from the case of those who claim that our bishops are not the great luminaries of learning that they used to be. That learning is useful, even important, on the episcopal bench is not to be doubted. But the idea that the professional scholar is fitly employed in the office of bishop is of course an absurdity. From all that has been said here it will be gathered that what we lack is not scholarly bishops, but thinking bishops and, pre-eminently, christianly thinking bishops. To turn the office of Father-in-God into that of scholar is in its way no less a perversion than to turn it into that of administrator. It is a peculiarly English, probably even a peculiarly Anglican, confusion of thought to assume that the pursuit of learning is somehow of necessity a less secular activity than the pursuit of wealth. The scholar is not, by the mere fact of his scholarship, a more religious, more spiritual, less secular being than the administrator or the merchant. The idea that because a man is learned, especially in subjects appertaining to religion, he is therefore secure from the seductions of worldliness is a fallacy. The notion that learned men necessarily have the kind of spirituality and wisdom which give profundity to their words and works is a deceptive myth bred in the nineteenth-century varsity common-rooms and now kept anachronistically alive by Crockford.

Indeed, though it is slightly beside the point in the present context to say so, the whole question of learning and ecclesiastical office needs to be thrashed out in the light of twentieth-century conditions. We are fifty years out of date in much of our thinking on this issue. We hear the archaic complaint that deaneries and canonries, like bishoprics, are no longer in the hands of scholars; that cathedral closes no longer produce a stream of learned tomes, theological and archaeological. Of course not. The vast development of our educational system is such that we have not — or ought not to have — theological scholars to spare for our cathedral closes. They are wanted in our universities, colleges, and grammar schools. There are not enough to go round. Why on earth should the Church consider it her duty to subsidize scholars and writers of books in cathedral closes when the State is willing and happy to employ them in universities and training colleges and schools? Accept the fact that scholarship is provided for elsewhere. The scholars should be holding the professorships and lectureships and the numerous appropriate jobs in publishing, editing, reviewing, and so on. There is vastly more scope for them than there was a hundred years ago. It is time for cathedral closes to be populated by priests with an entirely different bent. The way to use fruitfully the resources of the modern cathedral close is a problem that should be thought about at once: and it should be thought about christianly, not secularly. That is to say, all preconceptions about the social status, the hierarchical dignities of residentiary canons should be discounted. Likewise all prejudices preserving cathedral closes as miniature garden estates for the superannuated middle classes should be laid aside. We cannot afford these museum pieces, even as tourist attractions. It is not the Church's business to provide oases of picture-postcard dreamland for the delectation of faded gentility. Let us see, perhaps, houses for slum orphans under the shelter of our cathedral walls. (We have been ready enough to provide there schools for the sons of the privileged rich, whose exclusive doors are shut in the faces of aspiring workers.) In other words, let us think christianly about what should be happening under the shelter of our cathedrals. One would like to see at least one cathedral close as the home of a religious community.

What has been said here about our failure to think christianly over such matters as the appointment of bishops may easily be misunderstood. Our attack is directed upon mental attitudes within the Church. But of course to think christianly is to take into account the fact that God frequently overrules human intentions, especially in the religious sphere where prayer is constantly offered to him. Thus, though we have the right to say that our thinking has become secularized even in such matters as the choice of bishops, we have no right to conclude that God has never brought good out of evil in this respect. In other words, we may choose for bishop the wrong man on the wrong grounds by the wrong machinery; yet God may make something of that man in answer to the prayers and needs of his Church which at least diminishes the effect of human error and sin. To the secularist this argument is nonsensical. To him it is as though we had made a strong case and then run treacherously away from it at the last moment. If you think christianly to the end, you will always have surprises for the secularist—and often disappointments.

But—and this is a monstrously important "but"— though God may turn our evil and erring acts to some good account when we have sinned and erred in the confusion of ignorance and misunderstanding or when the prayers of others have weighed against our intentions, that in no way excuses sin and error. And once we have realized the evil or the error in a given mode of action, it would be wickedly perverse to continue with that mode of action on the grounds that God can bring good out of evil.

I have endeavoured in this chapter to show that to think christianly is a very different thing from thinking secularly about Christian matters. I have used the issue of the function and appointment of bishops to illustrate my thesis, both because it is a topical and controversial one upon which I felt certain things could be usefully said, and because it is one on which secular thinking has tended to swamp Christian thinking to a damaging degree. In pressing home and illustrating my basic distinction, I have necessarily given evidence of some of the presuppositions which distinguish the Christian mind's frame of reference from that of the secular mind. It is now appropriate to give a more systematic account of the nature of the Christian mind.

But first I must remark that the following chapters are obviously not intended to provide an exhaustive account of the Christian mind. To formulate all the presuppositions which constitute the educated Christian's proper frame of reference and to pursue deductions from each through their numerous ramifications in various fields of knowledge and experience would be an encyclopaedic task. Naturally I have selected a few significant marks of the Christian mind, and therefore it is reasonable that I should explain the basis of my selection. Briefly I have tried to balance the following considerations. Firstly, I have tried to look at some of those marks of the Christian mind which most deeply and gravely separate it from the secular mind, and especially at some of those marks which are at this moment notably inimical to the drift of contemporary thinking. Secondly, I have tried to consider some of those marks of the Christian mind which are not only alien to contemporary secularism, but are also ignored or neglected within the Church itself through the infectious influence of that secularism. Thirdly, I have tried to avoid redundant repetition of points made fully and plainly elsewhere. Thus, for instance, in spite of the intrinsic importance and relevance of the subject, I have not inserted here a chapter on the Christian mind's acute sensitivity to Providence, for the very good reason that I have written a full book on that subject (*The Will and the Way*).

PART TWO

The Marks of the Christian Mind

1

ITS SUPERNATURAL ORIENTATION

A PRIME MARK of the Christian mind is that it cultivates the eternal perspective. That is to say, it looks beyond this life to another one. It is supernaturally orientated, and brings to bear upon earthly considerations the fact of Heaven and the fact of Hell.

In this respect the religious view of life differs so fundamentally and comprehensively from the secular view of life that it seems scarcely possible for the Christian to communicate intelligibly with the modern secularist. And indeed this is our most acute problem to-day. It seems virtually impossible to bridge the gap between ourselves and our unbelieving fellow-men so as to present to them, vividly and convincingly, the Christian view of the human situation.

The Christian mind sees human life and human history held in the hands of God. It sees the whole universe sustained by his power and his love. It sees the natural order as dependent upon the supernatural order, time as contained within eternity. It sees this life as an inconclusive experience, preparing us for another; this world as a temporary place of refuge, not our true and final home.

But outside the sphere of Christian thinking there is a totally different view of things. Modern secular thought ignores the reality beyond this world. It treats this world as The Thing. Secularism is, by its very nature, rooted in this world, accounting it the only sure basis of knowledge, the only reliable source of meaning and value. Secularism puts its trust in this life and makes earthly happiness and well-being its primary concern.

The modern rejection of Christianity, rooted as it is in a hard-boiled secularism, has at its heart a total failure to sense the dependence of man, the creatureliness of man. Its most basic presupposition, implicit in all its judgements, is that this which we experience directly with the senses constitutes the heart and totality of things. Hence the collision between the Christian Faith and contemporary secular culture. For all teaching of Christian revelation deals with the breaking-in of the greater supernatural order upon our more limited finite world. That conception is at the heart of the doctrine of the Incarnation. It is at the heart of every claim to individual experience of God's love and power. The Greater breaks in upon the Smaller. But if our world here is seen as the totality of things, or even as the dominant sphere of existence, then the notion of the Greater breaking in upon it cannot be entertained. If *This World = All that Is*, then there is no *Greater-than-It* to break in upon it. The idea of God can be entertained only if you have first thought of man as someone than whom there could be Someone greater; only if you have first thought of the universe as something than which there could be Something more stable and important. Secularism is so rooted in this world that it does not allow for the existence of any other. Therefore whenever secularism encounters the Christian mind, either the Christian mind will momentarily shake that rootedness, or secularism will seduce the Christian mind to a temporary mode of converse which overlooks the supernatural.

For the truths of Christian revelation, one and all, put this life decisively within the framework of a bigger one; and the Christian mind, thinking christianly, cannot for a moment escape a frame of reference which reaches out to the supernatural.

In this respect the Christian mind has allowed itself to be subtly secularized by giving a purely *chronological* status to the eternal. That is to say, the Christian has relegated the significance of the eternal to the life that succeeds this one. In doing so, it has enabled itself to come to terms with the secular mind on a false basis. The basis is that here and now Christians and secularists can share the same conceptions, attitudes, and modes of action within the temporal sphere, since the essential difference between them—i.e. the dispute whether or not there is God's eternity beyond this world—is one which begins to be applicable only when this life is ended.

We are not suggesting that arguments of this kind are consciously articulated. They are not. We are trying to capture in words the sly process by which the Christian mind dechristianizes itself in this respect without intending to do so. Its conscious motives are good. It wants to operate in harmony with the secular mind wherever possible. Thus over laudable ventures in fruitful fields of activity—social, cultural, educational, political—the Christian comes to terms with the secularist. He argues thus: "This venture is a worthy one. These secularists are engaged in it because they are good men with high ideals anxious to serve a humanitarian purpose. Christians can co-operate with them because their work is good." Thus the Christian reasons and he acts accordingly. But, in co-operating with secularists the Christian necessarily, for all practical purposes, ceases to proclaim that in his eyes this work is God's work undertaken in God's name, for God's people, in God's world. He will put into the background of his mind, when questions of policy or practice are to be discussed with the secularists, the fact that this humanitarian work is for him part of a gigantic battle between good and evil which splits the universe. He will keep quiet about the temporariness of this life, the insecurity of earthly fortune, the ceaseless creaturely dependence of man upon that which is beyond this world.

The Christian works side by side with the secularist. He prays sincerely in private about his work. But for practical day-to-day purposes he does not talk christianly about aims, plans, and policies, because he is talking to secularists. In other words, his mind ceases, at the level of communication, to think christianly. Indeed the Christian *trains* his mind, *forces* it, to think secularly—so as to help the job in hand to be done efficiently. In this way, by gradual stages, the Christian loses the habit of thinking christianly over the field of practical affairs in which he is actively involved. Setting out with the charitable aim of co-operating with good secularist activities, the Christian has slowly divested himself of the habit of thinking christianly and acquired the habit of thinking secularly, except in reference to his personal spiritual life and his private moral code.

Hence the modern Christian, a schizophrenic type who hops in and out of his Christian mentality as the topic of conversation changes from the Bible to the day's newspaper, or the field of action changes from Christian Stewardship to commercial advertising, or the environment changes from the vestry to the office. No doubt the laity are more schizophrenic than the parish priests. On the other hand observation suggests that bishops and other high dignitaries are more schizophrenic than either.

This charge needs to be explained. One may be frankly and overtly schizophrenic, or one may blanket the duality. Thus the Christian layman who joins in the secular meeting may very well say to himself: "It's no good talking about the Kingdom of Heaven or eternal salvation to these chaps to-day. It's very vital to the work in question. Indeed for me, privately speaking, it's crucial. But for them it's meaningless. There's a common job to do that is worth doing. So I'll forget about that kind of thing for the time being." Now this kind of thinking is not perhaps excusable: but it is certainly understandable. It results in Christian silence. The particular discussion and action go forward in the absence of specifically Christian thinking—with no infusion from the Christian mind. But note: no one imagines, no one pretends that Christian thinking has contributed at the conscious level to the total venture.

Perhaps the nature of our charge against higher ecclesiastical dignitaries is now becoming clear. By the very nature of their position, they are involved officially —on platforms, on committees, as chairmen, as over-seers—in many laudable activities dominated by secular thinking, of an educational, social, or cultural kind. In the discussion of practical affairs these dignitaries find themselves in exactly the same position as the schizo-phrenic Christian layman. No one else is thinking in terms of an earthly life played out in time against the background of eternity with the issue of salvation as its dominating concern. So the bishop pushes that kind of thing to the back of his mind and joins the discussion with a mind operating within the accepted secular frame of reference. But there is a difference. As a

71

bishop, by virtue of his office, of his known ecclesiastical dignity, he feels it his inescapable duty to drag in the Christian overtone. It may be merely that he says a brief prayer at the beginning of the meeting. Or it may be that he remarks how the Church is very concerned about this or that social problem too. Or it may be that he inserts the odd pious platitude—"I'm sure God's blessing will be upon this" or "We must all pray that this will succeed". Whatever it is, the final result is, if I am right, an unfortunate one. For the impression is left that here *the Church has made its contribution*, that the Christian view has been heard along with others, that in fact the Christian mind has been at work.

The frankly schizophrenic layman makes no pretence and gives no impression of having brought the Christian mind to bear upon the secular venture. But the bishop, or other dignitary, is involved in a pretence. The effect of his action is that everybody assumes, and talks as though, the Christian mind has been at work, when in fact its operation has as usual been forcibly suppressed. This may well become a more and more urgent matter as the tide of secularism swells. It is time that our bishops and higher clergy, cushioned as they are by status from many of the frustrations of parish priests and laity, re-examined very carefully the ventures to which they ought to give authoritative official support and the manner in which that support ought to be given. Otherwise the situation, already not unknown, will more frequently develop, in which humbler Churchmen are striving to introduce an element of Christian thinking into various activities of our culture, whilst from the ecclesiastical heights the false impression is being officially conveyed that these activities already go forward under the impetus of a thoroughly Christian purpose.

72

It needs no argument to prove that the supernaturally orientated view of the human situation proper to the Christian mind is remote indeed from the view nourished by secular culture. This is most clearly shown at the popular level. Turn to the glossy magazines, to the sensational press, to the cinema, T.V., and the like. Ask yourself what kind of a world is pictured there. Is it the world known vividly to the Christian mind? A world in which angel and demon are locked in conflict? A world packed full of sinners desperately dependent upon the mercy of God? A world amok with fundamentally powerless creatures, running hither and thither, foolishly imagining that they can do without God, and making an appalling mess of things as a result? A world voyaging like a little vessel across the sea of time, taking its passengers to their final home? A world fashioned by God, sustained by God, worried over by God, died for by God?

Is that the world represented by our Press and radio and T.V., our journalists and politicians? No. The secular mind has a totally conflicting view of our world and our situation in it. The world pictured by modern secularism and present to current popular thinking is very different. It is a self-sufficient world. It is a world whose temporality is conclusive and final, whose comprehensiveness of experience embraces all that is and that will ever be. It is a world run by men, possessed by men, dominated by men, its course determined by men. It is a world in which men have got things taped. The secular mind feels that things are, on the whole, under control. There may be temporary difficulties of course—like the East-West tension—but we're doing pretty well on the whole. Witness our rising standard of living, our highly organized civilization, our social services and the like.

The Christian mind looks at the propaganda of modern secularism and is astonished to learn that under man's management the world is supposed to be on the whole in a tolerable shape. The normal course through life is pictured as a progress through an increasing number of acquisitions and comforts. You get a house, then you get a fridge, then you get a telly, then you get a car; and all the time you are peacefully maturing, with a pretty young wife at your side, from youth to early middle age. For in the world of advertisements no man ever grows older than thirty-five and no woman grows older than twenty-seven. It is a cosy picture of life, full of colour and ease. There is always plenty to eat and drink. The furniture never gets old or drab. The wall-paper never peels off the walls. The sun shines. The gardens appear to weed themselves. There is no pain, except for a fleeting hint of indigestion which can be magically whisked away by the right pills.

The Christian mind is shocked, bewildered, and, as it seems, rendered impotent to communicate meaning-fully with a secular mind so cut off from its dearest and most illuminating presuppositions. Therefore the Christian mind instinctively withdraws, turns its attention to other matters — say, the individual spiritual life, or the problem of Church disunity.

Of all the marks of the Christian mind, its super-natural orientation is the most important for anyone considering the collision of the Christian mind with the secular mind in the modern world. For it is the rooted-ness of the secular mind in the natural order which produces the most fundamental and violent clash with specifically Christian thinking. This is true at all levels, from the scholarly level at which rationalists or positi-vists collide with theologians, to the popular level at which the glossy magazine picture of life closes the blinkered mind to the Church's account of the human situation. Nevertheless the attention given to this topic in the present book is intentionally limited. That is because I have already investigated in detail elsewhere many aspects of this particular collision between the Christian mind and the secular mind, and more especially the process by which the Christian mind can be secularized by the weakening of its supernatural orientation. (See *The Faith and Modern Error*.)

But we cannot escape the necessity of summing up at this point some of the crucial differentiae of the Christian mind as endowed with the eternal perspective.

The Christian mind's realization that all is not over when you die is something which affects not only the future but the present. To believe that men will be called to account for each wrong committed and each good committed is itself enough to give an urgency to human deliberations and decisions which the secular mind cannot sense. When one weighs the full momentousness of this particular distinction between the Christian mind and the secular mind, one is awestruck. What price are we paying, in terms of intellectual clarity and integrity, for the continuance of easy co-existence of the Christian mind with the secular mind? Ponder the violence of the concealed collision. On the one hand is the assumption that all is over when you die; that after sixty or seventy years, sheltered and cushioned by the Welfare State, you can sign off for good; that eating, sleeping, growing, learning, breeding, and the rest, constitute the total sum of things; that in worldly prosperity and well-being lies the source of all meaning and value. On the other hand is the almost crushing awareness of a spiritual war tearing at the heart of the

universe, pushing its ruthless way into the lives of men —
stabbing at you now, now, now, in the impulses and
choices of every waking moment; the belief that the
thoughts and actions of every hour are moulding a soul
which is on its way to eternity; that we are choosing
every moment of our lives in obedience or disobedience
to the God who created and sustains all that is; that we
are always responsible, always at war, always involved
in what is spiritual and deathless; that we are committing
ourselves with every breath to salvation or damnation.

Do we, as Christians, mentally inhabit the world
presented to us by the faith of the Church as the real
world? Do we mentally inhabit a world with a Heaven
above it and a Hell beneath it; a world in which man is
called to live daily, hourly, in contact with the God
whom neither time nor space can limit? Do we, as
Christians, mentally inhabit an order of being which is
superior to decay and death?

This book is not about Christian behaviour, but
Christian thinking. I do not ask what is our moral
condition, but what is our mental condition. The question is, do we in our *thinking* generally take into account
the Christian view of life's significance as exemplified
above? Do we bring this kind of picture of the human
situation to bear upon our discussion of human affairs,
allowing it to determine our contribution to the secular
activities in which we are involved? Do we, in this
respect, *think* christianly? The truth is that for the most
part we don't. Our personality may bear the imprint of
our attempts to live the spiritual life. Our moral conduct may be determined by the Christian code. But,
generally speaking, we fail completely to introduce into
the mental and deliberative life of society a strain of
thinking wholly coloured by that *tinta* which bespeaks a

supernatural orientation. In short we ensure that there shall be no vigorous Christian mind helping to determine the character of contemporary culture.

The collision between the Christian mind and a solidly earthbound culture ought to be a violent one. In fact the impact does not occur; for the Christian lays aside the presuppositions proper to a supernaturally orientated personality when he steps outside the sphere of specifically religious activity or of personal morality. He speaks the language of secularism.

The Church's present neglect of the intellectual element in modern life may prove to be a very costly one. And by "intellectual element" I mean, not only the activity of professional intellectuals from which theology is so notably absent, but also the mental activity which goes on in the minds of all men as a background and basis for their practical decisions and activities. The bland assumption that the Church's life will continue to be fruitful so long as we go on praying and cultivating our souls, and irrespective of whether we trouble to think and talk christianly, and therefore theologically, about anything which we or others may do or say, may turn out to have dire results. Already the deference shown to Christian attitudes is wearing thin in some circles. The conventional polite allowance that at least "there must be *something* in it—*something* behind the line these Christians take" is made with increasing grudgingness. The suspicion grows apace that our inhibiting slogans are mere postures concealing an arid emptiness, mere expressions of an irrational resistance to progress.

This is not an attack upon the Church. We grant that in many fields of activity our Church is alive and busy. One can point to parishes where the faithful worship dutifully, where fellowship is strong and vital, where devout priests are preoccupied with the pastoral and spiritual care of their people. There, one can say, the Church is about its proper work. It is bringing God's people to our Lord in regular worship and prayer; it is exhorting them to live the Christian life. Then again, our Church speaks wisely on many questions of personal morality. And it provides the nourishment and the environment by which men can be disciplined in the spiritual life. There is no lack of clear leadership and direction to us in our efforts to root our personal lives in our Lord's by the practice of prayer and meditation.

But, amid all this ferment of social and pastoral activity, of ethical and spiritual exhortation, the mind of modern man is neglected and forgotten. For the Christian mind is no longer cultivated. The Christian mind is too provocative, too dangerous, too revolutionary perhaps. If nourished, if fed fat on the milk of the word, it will perhaps collide so violently with the secular mind which dominates our comfortable and complacent set-up that we Christians shall find ourselves, mentally at least, persecuted again.

We prefer to let sleeping dogs lie, and shut our eyes to the price that may have to be paid for neglect. It will not be the penalty of persecution. Nothing so noble as martyrdom, even mental martyrdom. The reward of our neglect will be *their* neglect: indifference, the averted eyes and turned heads of those who have no longer the time to listen to mere sentimentalists. And if, too late, we challenge the secularists for an explanation of why the Church is now ignored, the reply will be a simple and clear one—"My dear fellow, your Christian morality is fine up to a point: for centuries it has saved us from barbarism. Your Christian

78

spiritual culture is a remarkable phenomenon: certainly it has extended the reach of human penetration as remarkably as did the great mysticisms of the East. Your Christian fellowship is often wonderfully healing and healthy: it has enriched the lives of many who in the pre-psychiatric period might have succumbed to frustration and pain. . . . But of course all these things are invalid; for your central teachings are wholly incredible, your theology a tangle of outmoded obscurantist metaphysics, your basic doctrines utterly discredited, your view of man's situation and destiny totally incompatible with modern knowledge."

The danger that we shall find ourselves, not in isolated instances, but as a general and accepted feature of life, face to face with this kind of charge, is not remote. It is made all the more menacing by our steady failure to think christianly; by our quiet suppression, in deference to secularism, of those who would bring theology into every committee room and classroom and office like a banner.

A resistance stirs within us. Do we *want* our theology paraded thus? As natural men, no. We do not want it any more than we want the discipline of the Christian moral code, the discipline of penitence, the painful call to self-surrender. But if it is the intellectual expression of that Faith by which we live, how can our minds work christianly without it?

Wherever men think and talk, the banner will have to be raised. Not, of course, for the purpose of pursuing a ceaseless propaganda campaign, but for the purpose of pursuing clarity and integrity. Not that we should convert, but that we should be understood. Not that the Christian mind should become the immediate and overwhelming vehicle of all truth to all men, but that the

79

Christian mind should be recognized for what it is: something different, something distinctive, something with depth, hardness, solidity; a pleasure to fight with and a joy to be beaten by.

If the day comes when the Church is no longer listened to where men meet to nourish and sharpen the intellect, the struggle to establish a Christian culture will have been lost. If to-day the Church is silent and inert at those points of our civilization where the thinking of the age is hammered into shape, where decisions are made and actions planned, or where the minds of future generations are moulded, its influence upon the twentieth-century will be rotted at the core. The Catholic tradition of our Church is that the Christian life is a life for the full man. There is no room in Christendom for a culture of the spirit which neglects the mind, for a discipline of the will which by-passes the intellect. It may be that the dominant evil of our time is neither the threat of nuclear warfare nor the mechanization of society, but the disintegration of human thought and experience into separate unrelated compartments. For a feature of the diseased condition of modern society is the parcelling out of human faculties—physical, emotional, intellectual, spiritual—into distinct categories, separately exploited, separately catered for. Man is dismembered. In the high incidence of mental disease you can measure something of the cost of this dismemberment. In so far as the Church nurtures the schizophrenic Christian, the Church herself contributes to the very process of dismemberment which it is her specific business to check and counter. For the Church's function is properly to reconstitute the concept and the reality of the full man, faculties and forces blended and united in the service of God. The

Church's mission as the continuing vehicle of divine incarnation is precisely that—to build and rebuild the unified Body made and remade in the image of the Father. The mind of man must be won for God.

One is tempted at this point to list those topics and activities which assume a different aspect when there is brought to bear upon them a mind which reckons, not just with time, but with eternity; not just with human life-spans, but with destinies beyond the grave. In fact, of course, the list would be endless. It is clear, for instance, that any issue or activity which touches upon death will assume a different appearance and character when viewed in the light of an eternal perspective. Thus such controversial topics and activities as those of war, capital punishment, euthanasia, suicide, the use of life-prolonging drugs, and indeed the whole of medical practice and ethos, will inevitably look different to the mind surveying the human scene in the light of eternity. The dispute whether death is the end of all known and assured existence or the beginning of a life surer and less confined will inevitably provoke conflicting attitudes to the topics mentioned above. But, in a sense, death is relevant to every human issue, every earthly activity, since it raises the question of the significance and status of all that transpires terrestrially. And if death is universally relevant, then it follows that the Christian's eternal perspective is universally relevant too.

Obviously, for instance, the eternal perspective totally alters the character of suffering, failure, destruction—anything which seems, in one way or another, to knock the bottom out of earthly life. Disease and suffering, in so far as they reduce man's total experience of

81

existence here to something not worth having in itself, cannot be reconciled with the demand of the human mind for justice and meaning in things, unless there is that beyond this life and outside this world which both compensates for suffering and transforms its total significance. When you contemplate the spectacle of a girl almost wholly paralysed as a result of a car accident, say, and condemned to a life of near total immobility, speechlessness, blindness, you will see the tragedy either as the last word in that poor creature's knowledge and taste of being, or as something which is to be swept away beyond death in a new, richer, fuller life. In the former case, you will surely wish only to tear the universe in pieces. In the latter case, you will surely know that the only thing to do is to pray.

The experience of physical disease and disability, the frustration of fine efforts and aspirations, the disappointment of long-cherished hopes—all these experiences, common and fundamental to human life, have their essential character and meaning determined for us and for all men by whether they are thought about christianly or secularly—whether they are conceived against the background of a limited finite existence which is but the prelude to eternity, or against the background of a human course on earth that is finally and exclusively man's full destiny.

But, of course, just as the eternal perspective transforms the character of anything which touches on death, of anything which is sad, painful, or disastrous—war, famine, earthquake, sickness, insanity—so too the eternal perspective transforms the character of earthly success, prosperity, and pleasure.

For the Christian mind earthly well-being is not the *summum bonum*, as pain and death are not the worst evil.

Eternal well-being is the final aim and end of things here. This means that success and prosperity within the earthly set-up cannot be regarded as a final criterion. Nor indeed can happiness within time be regarded as a final criterion.

The overriding and comprehensive aims of the Christian mind thus clash violently with those of the secular mind: their judgements upon particular human affairs conflict correspondingly. On the one hand, say, the secular mind's reasoning about nuclear war is often determined by the proposition that the destruction of civilization and perhaps of human life on this planet would be in itself the last and final evil — beyond which nothing. On the other hand the secular mind's reasoning about, say, divorce and remarriage is largely determined by the presupposition that individual happiness during life on this planet is the only sure well-being, and that there can be no binding obligations which conflict with its demands.

We have now established that the Christian mind, by cultivating the eternal perspective, will bring a totally different frame of reference to bear upon all that touches human success or human failure, human joy or human misery, human health or human pain. In short there is nothing in our experience which will not look different to the Christian mind than to the secular mind. And many of the issues and activities which will be most vitally transformed by being regarded christianly are precisely those which are with us now as constant topics of public controversy — war, crime, delinquency, disease, divorce, insanity, vice. The question what is to be done about these problems is a very different question faced christianly and faced secularly, in that the pursuit of temporal well-being gives a twist to human thinking which the pursuit of eternal well-being will not always condone or permit. Fortunately, of course, practical programmes can often be hit upon which Christian and secularist can alike approve—if sometimes for different reasons. It is plain that the best treatment for appendicitis or tuberculosis is determined by technical considerations into which philosophical or theological presuppositions do not enter—except at the almost universally agreed level of such platitudes as, It is better to heal than not to heal. But, on the other hand, the question of what is the best method of dealing with prostitution or homosexuality could not be settled, even at the immediate practical level, on the basis only of an agreed technology.

The dominant concern in this book is that there is no living Christian dialogue on most of the topics just mentioned. Or, if you like, that no stream of Christian thinking flows recognizably into the secular dialogues now being carried on. By and large, we have to admit that there is no general awareness in our society of a prevalent mentality that would bring to bear upon all the gravest issues of our time the perspective of eternity. When the Christian speaks, to the subject of war, delinquency, disease, vice, and so on, we do not find that the audience stirs itself and prepares to hear something *different*, prepares to listen to a mind which will flood the topic of controversy with that distinct and distinctive light which must always flow from bringing into view a new dimension—the dimension of eternity.

We have become afraid of our own convictions. And our fear has not been, in this respect, a wholly unworthy one. History has been full of warnings against the damage which fanatical dogmatists can do to human

84

society and to the Church itself. No men more loudly and impressively than the officers of the Holy Inquisition claimed that temporal well-being must be subordinated to eternal well-being; that physical pain and earthly suffering were as nothing when weighed in the balance against the damnation of a soul. One might go further and say that no body of men more strenuously strove to preserve the distinctness and distinctiveness of the Christian mind. We have perhaps been frightened too much by horrors of that kind. It is because the devil is an angel that his evil power is so poisonous. It is because the inquisitors had a crucial element of truth mixed up with their dismal self-deceptions that the perversions they represented were so diabolical.

Twentieth-century Christendom errs and no doubt will continue to err — but it will not err in the direction of the Inquisition. Rather, through reacting against excessive dogmatism, against exclusiveness, against withdrawal from the proper activities of the world, it may destroy through a too yielding compliance with secularism, a too easy commerce of mind with mind, that powerful and lucid rational construction which constitutes its divinely guaranteed estimate of life.

2

ITS AWARENESS OF EVIL

W E HAVE said that the Christian mind thinks in terms of Heaven and Hell. In other words it is conscious of the universe as a battlefield between the forces of good and evil. It follows that the Christian mind has an acute and sensitive awareness of the power and spread of evil upon the human scene.

The Church sums up, in the doctrine of Original Sin, the fact that men and women are drawn towards evil by weaknesses in their fallen nature. The magnitude and variety of the evil forces waiting to ensnare the human soul are hinted at in the triple formulation, the World, the Flesh, and the Devil. If anyone needs to be convinced that the Church's view of human nature and the human situation is neither a sentimental nor a rose-tinted one, let him read through the Book of Common Prayer, and note how often it refers to man's desperate struggle against the powers of evil.

The notion that this world, and the powers of it, are in the grip of evil, is too well established in Christian teaching to be lightly disregarded, yet Christians have grown accustomed to shrug off the more sombre implications of this truth. We have inoculated ourselves against sensitive realization of the world's evil.

By "the world" I mean what the Church has always meant by "the world"—and this surely includes the official and respectable earthly set-up, the thing ruled over by the Powers-that-be; indeed (there is no escaping the word) what we now call "the Establishment". This needs to be said, for we have now sufficiently secularized our minds to be in the habit of viewing the social and political set-up in which we are involved as something wholly, or largely, good in the eyes of God. We have kept alive our Christian urge to discriminate between good and evil by the convenient device of labelling our own institutions good and those of our past enemies, or potential enemies, as evil. In this way we manage both to eat our cake and to have it. We complacently absolve ourselves from passing judgement on the set-up which nourishes us so comfortably. We lean back in our armchairs, toast our toes by the electric fire, turn on the radio or the telly, and indulge in the righteous pleasure of learning how much evil there is in the world—elsewhere.

We deceive ourselves with our own conjuring trick. Yet we ought not to be able to get away with it thus. A living Christian mind, with a keen and cutting edge, would surely have saved us from our cruder complacencies. That we should sit so smugly in judgement upon the materialism of the Soviets—we in a country whose political parties, Left and Right alike, have, morally speaking, abdicated. Both parties woo us by telling us, in different ways, that if we support them they will further improve our material comforts. Did not the present government come to power on the claim, "Vote for us and we will double your standard of living in the next twenty years"? And was there a powerful Christian voice which replied: "Not on your life. Do something for the standard of living of the Indians, the Asiatics, or those Egyptians whom you so recently tried to blast with your bombs"? The Church can never truly

87

ally itself either with our materialistic Conservatism or our materialistic Socialism. For the Church is up against the Establishment—inevitably, by the very nature of the Church and the very nature of the Establishment. It always was. It was the Establishment that crucified our Lord. You can be quite sure that the first-century equivalents of our respectable publicity organs were solidly behind that bit of tidying-up on Pontius Pilate's part.

Of course the Church has not been wholly silent about the evils mentioned here. Sometimes fine words have been spoken. One thinks of Trevor Huddleston, a man alive with the kind of moral leadership our civilization desperately needs. One can thank God a hundred times that he was made Bishop of Masasi. One could have thanked God a thousand times, had he been given an even more influential position.

I am suggesting that the Church's alliance with the secular Establishment is too close in that the Church has tended to accept secularism's own doctored version of the current struggle between good and evil, a version which has two faces, the international face and the national face. The one face is that which shows the good West locked in a moral contest with the evil, materialistic East. The other face is that which shows at home the good benevolent government vainly trying to suppress the multifarious evil forces represented by bank-raiders, prostitutes, perverts, juvenile delinquents, wild-cat strikers, red trade-unionists, teddy-boys, drunken drivers, sit-down demonstrators, sex-maniacs, shop-stewards, and Jehovah's Witnesses who refuse to have blood-transfusions. No one can deny that it is in these terms that the Establishment, through its various agencies of publicity, represents the current struggle between good and evil. This would scarcely matter to us in the present context, were it not that Christians seem happy to swallow this version of the good–evil conflict hook, line, and sinker. There is a depressing amount of evidence, in sermons and in letters to the Press for instance, that Christian clergy and laity are ready to accept the secular Establishment's own cosy view of the current battles in the age-long struggle between good and evil. The voice of the Church is heard, joining in the current dialogue about Soviet intransigence, industrial unrest, or prostitution, and the frame of reference set up by secularist discourse is fully preserved. That widening out of the issue and that bringing home to roost of the glib accusation—both so typical of our Lord's pronouncements—one does not hear. In such easy compliance one can measure the blunting of Christian sensibilities and the decay of the Christian mind.

The true Christian mind will bring to bear upon the human scene those specifically Christian moral criteria which by no amount of casuistry can be equated with the generally accepted respectability-morality of our day. In the Christian moral system the key sin is pride—that perversion of the will by which the self is asserted as the centre of the universe. That is the mark of the utterly lost soul; an established and constant habit of manipulating all people and all interests in the service of the self. Likewise the key virtue in the Christian moral system is obedience; that self-commitment in thought and act by which God is asserted as centre of the universe. That is the hall-mark of the Christian moral life; a persisting and cheerful effort to make of all life's activities and relationships a fit offering to God.

Now it is plain that, on the negative side (that is, in

89

respect of many of its prohibitions) there is a good deal of overlap between the Christian moral code and the accepted morality of contemporary secularism. The crimes which produce public disgrace—theft, embezzlement, murder, rape, living on immoral earnings, and so on—are as hateful to the Christian as they are contrary to the law. Indeed each of these crimes has the evil character we have described, of manipulating people and interests in the service of the self. But the Christian mind cannot accept the facile distinction made by the secular mind—reflected in secular publicity—between the nation's criminals and libertines on the one hand and her good men on the other. For the discerning Christian knows that a cunning or intelligent man may lead a life of almost diabolical pride, in which he strives in every moment to minister to the desires and vanities of his own inflated self—and yet may pass for a respectable, law-abiding citizen. Indeed he may rise to a position of eminence in the world by the persistent and subtle practice of the most calculated self-service. He may become a judge, packing off poor men to gaol with words of stern condemnation ostensibly reflecting the indignation of righteous men, and yet he may be, by virtue of a cancerous inner self-centredness, the greatest sinner, essentially the most evil man, ever to have entered the courtroom in which he sits—though its dock has accommodated a stream of murderers, thieves, and perverts for the last fifty years. The Christian mind *cannot overlook this possibility.* Not that the Christian *likes* to reflect thus—reminding himself that not only the world's great ones, but he himself, may be far more sinful, far more eaten up by evil, than this man trembling in the dock, condemned to life imprisonment, pilloried in the Press, a byword in the conversation of the whole nation. It isn't a comforting train of thought. The Christian no more wants to be troubled by it than the secularist would. But the Christian mind—if it has not been numbed into almost total insensitivity—will not allow him to forget it. The Christian mind knows that, in any sorting out of the sheep and the goats, of the virtuous from the sinful, the forces of Heaven would slice through human society at an unexpected angle. The knife would cut firmly, but certainly not horizontally. What can we say or think of how it would separate the self-seekers from the fundamentally God-directed souls, except that it would certainly not leave all the convicts and perverts and public nuisances on one side, and all the cabinet ministers and business executives and members of the Watch Committee on the other?

There is nothing—not even priesthood, episcopacy, or a religious profession—which cannot be perverted into a mere means of appeasing a hungry vanity, into an instrument of constant self-service. In an age in which the Church over the world has made a staggeringly compliant compromise with secularism we have special reason to recall the elementary revolutionary paradoxes of the Christian Message. The last shall be first and the first shall be last. A poor woman, who has perhaps even done time in gaol for petty theft, and whose religious activities are restricted to hurried daily prayers and a snatched occasional faithfulness at the altar, may go through a life of scraping and scrubbing and comparative squalor to wake up one day a saint. (For so much she did was done in obedience.) While a brilliant divine may give his thoughts to religious study every day of his life, and write the most perceptive theological treatise of his age, only to wake up one day, in time or out of time, to the realization that it was all done in furtive self-service. (For the Judgement will show him this if he does not learn it before.)

The Christian mind, were it alive, would be continually overthrowing the moral judgements of the secular world — probing the moral poses so readily assumed with a penetrating check on the readier condemnations. It is too easy for a man who has never known what it is to lack food or comfort, to pass judgement on a thief. It is too easy for a husband as heterosexual as a stallion to pass judgement on the paederast. It is too easy for the fulfilled businessman, whose pockets are laden and whose life is agog with stimulating and fruitful commercial competitiveness, to pass judgement on the ganging-up teenagers who desperately seek the thrusts and tensions of growth and rivalry in the drab backwaters of a now parcelled-out social fabric. It is far too easy, if you happen to have (by God's gift) a decent body and a decent brain, to bag a ladder and climb into a decentish sort of niche in this well buttressed society of ours, to adopt a nice statuesque pose, and then to start shying moral ammunition at all those easy targets that the Press and the cosy bourgeoisie will applaud you for attacking.

It is too easy. It is bad enough when headmasters and judges and cabinet ministers do it. When priests and bishops join in, one wants to scream aloud in protest. Not that the obvious wickednesses must not be judged. Of course they must. But the Christian mind will never leave off judging at the point where the breakers of the law and the dissidents of the Establishment have been probed and harried — while the respectably complacent have been left alone. We need the *tu quoque* and the *ego quoque* to complete the Christian judgement.

92

Yet in this society of ours, riddled with the vanities and indulgences of the rich and the successful, a bishop can find time to turn his big guns on Bingo. Bingo, if you please, in a society which boasts the Stock Exchange, take-over bids, the turning of £8,000 into £100,000 overnight by speculation in land. Bingo, which is about as wicked an occupation as teaching fleas to dance. Why, when you consider the relative opportunities for the exercise of pride and envy and uncharity in thought, word, and deed, there is probably less sin committed in a month of Bingo evenings than in a single meeting of the average parochial church council or a single vicarage garden-party.

Where is there evidence of the Christian mind at work in this field to-day, bringing home to the popular consciousness the gaping rift between the morality of comfortable secularism and the morality of the Cross? What sign is there of a vigorous Christian dialogue with the world, for ever highlighting, not the obvious sins, not the much-publicized immoralities, but the subtle, insidious evil which ensnares the hearts of the success-ful, respectable, established, applauded men and women—always surely the Devil's readiest prey?

Because the world is evil, its judgements are not to be relied upon. Hedging itself about with all the defences available, it will naturally produce a legal sys-tem sharply protective of its own interests. Thus one man is given ten years hard labour for robbing a bank of £20,000, while another man is given twelve months for savagely beating an infant child almost to the point of death. Of course the world's judgements are topsy-turvy. It is "the World". It speaks plainly to us from the pages of the morning paper. Whoso injureth a little child shall be moderately punished, but whoso robbeth

93

a bank of bits of paper, it were better that a millstone were hanged round his neck and he were thrown into the depths of the sea.

Without for a moment condoning evil of any kind, we have got to learn to distinguish, to discriminate, between the diamond-hard Christian ethic, and the soft code trimmed to buttress the securities of a materialistic society. The Christian mind will do this constantly; it will be unable to avoid doing it by virtue of the inescapable illumination of a developed conscience. Thus the Christian mind will bring naught for our comfort in its moral judgements—and naught for the comfort of any who feed fat on the well-hedged perquisites of a social system rigged in the interests of acquisitive fitters-in.

Because the world is "the World", because secularism is in the saddle, it follows that the Christian mind is suspicious of fashionable current conformities. The thinking Christian will not readily assume those modes of thought and behaviour by which one adapts oneself to the fashions prevailing in leading or influential social groups. The current conformities of the mind are those views and attitudes most congenial to dominant drifts in current thinking. To adopt the maximum current conformities is to equip oneself as fully as possible to climb the ladder of promotion, to make money, to rise in society, to "get on".

Since the predominant values of our secular society are materialistic, and its ideals this-worldly, in other words since our secular society remains generally untouched by the Christian leaven at work in it, it follows that any attempt to accommodate oneself wholly to the predominant notions and attitudes of that society will involve weakening that supernatural orientation which is fundamental to Christian thinking. In so far as certain notions and attitudes are cultivated as the right and proper ones to ensure promotion and acceptance in a society rootedly secular, they are inevitably suspect to the Christian mind. This is not to say that they are all bad. Rather it means that they are more likely to be bad than good. Since they are crucial elements in determining and sustaining that hierarchical structure of materialistic secularism which is perhaps, in strict moral terms, one of its most dangerous because most corrupting aspects, they are to be viewed with caution and subjected to close scrutiny.

Let us take a look at one or two current conformities of influential social groups. (We have of course already dealt with some without introducing the actual phrase.) There is, for instance, the notion that remarriage after divorce is something totally different from adultery. The Christian, however informed, is currently expected to talk as though it were different. He is expected, except in some undefined official capacity as a member of a society whose rules he can't do anything about, to *think* of remarriage after divorce as something totally different from adultery. He is asked to accept a distinction between unregistered adulterous liaisons and State-registered ones, that institutionalizes infidelity and converts morality into a licensing system. But the Christian mind cannot regard serial polygamy, indulged in over the years with the help of the divorce courts, as wildly different from contemporaneous polygamy. The respect for sheer time shown by the law in its distinction between bigamy and the remarriage of divorcees must strike the Christian as irrational. Indeed the Christian mind finds a logical absurdity in the tenacity with which the secular world clings officially to monogamy. Moreover the Christian mind, reflecting

95

coolly and dispassionately, is tempted to conclude that it would be easier to make a moral case for polygamy than for successive alliances punctuated by visits to the divorce court. If a man, well-established in middle life, wants to take a new wife, young and attractive, does he improve matters, or make them worse, by also throwing off the ageing wife he has lived with since youth? This is the sort of uncomfortable thinking which the Christian mind is likely to pursue, set free from the limits imposed by the ill-thought-out code of modern secularism. In theory polygamy is perhaps easier to defend than divorce and remarriage. In a polygamous household only *one* partner is promiscuous.

This illustration is not intended to provide a defence of polygamy. Rather it is intended to draw attention to the vast chasm separating the Christian mind from the secular mind in its moral thinking. To class repeated divorce and remarriage with polygamy is to the secular mind outrageous, to the Christian mind natural and logical.

Perhaps it is fair now to illustrate my point with a current notion of a more sophisticated kind. I select the idea, virtually unquestioned just now, that any discussion or literary exploitation of sexual matters, perversions, or aberrations, is good *provided that it is serious*. This idea meets us every week-end in the comments of highbrow, middlebrow, and lowbrow critics alike, on books, plays, films, radio, and television. It is regarded as healthy to describe or represent intercourse, promiscuity, vice, homosexuality, lesbianism, sadism, and the like, if you do so *seriously*. To put material of this kind before the public is "courageous" and "honest" if you do it *seriously*. Watching it or reading it is "adult" (and therefore good) if you do it *seriously*. The number of times the word *serious* occurred during the *Lady Chatterley's Lover* trial is significant. The high peak of the trial was a solemn moment when, before the awed and grave company in the court, Richard Hoggart uttered a well-known four-letter word with the gravity and reverence with which one might publicly speak the sacred name of our Lord.

I hope I am not casting off the Christian mind for a mentality far less regenerate when I say that I do not like this new seriousness. I do not like this new perverted puritanism which fanatically refuses to laugh at gutter words normally reserved for reference to our reproductive organs and functions viewed in their most purely animal aspect. This perverse prudery which would deny to the human race, burdened as it is with an excessively demanding sexuality, the safety valve of humour, could do great damage to our society. To have talk about romantic love (not to mention "holy communion") mixed up with the vocabulary of the lavatory wall is bad not only because it impairs the sacredness of the sacred but also because it impairs the earthiness of the earthy. Who are these people who would at once deny us the rich flavour of romantic love and the hearty salt of the bawdy? That Lawrence was, in a deep sense, a puritan need not be doubted. That the *Lady Chatterley* verdict was a victory for a new prudery, hard and unyielding, which has none of the mellow sensitivity of Victorian prudery, is equally certain. We are face to face with a new philistinism, grotesque and obtuse, which will keep its face rigidly straight over such a laughably bad book (I repeat *laughably* bad) as *Lady Chatterley's Lover*.

We all know that flowers grow best in manured soil. If that fact ever ceased to be paradoxical for us, our experience would be gravely impoverished. To bring together incongruous ideas and modes of expression for comic, paradoxical, or sensational purposes, may be justified. The comic or sensational quality resides in a full realization of their incongruity. But to bring incongruous ideas and modes of expression together in order to suggest that all experience and modes of expression are of a piece, is to fly in the face of life itself; to deny the richly varied character of our universe; to deny the remarkable subtlety of our ranging sensitivities; to mutilate our whole machinery of response to experience.

The sense of humour is fundamental to our sense of proportion and therefore to our very rationality. No argument is needed to stress that humour is a bulwark against despair and insanity. It is not a coincidence that the same modern movement which would flood our cultural life with stark revelations of sexuality reveals itself so basically deficient in a sense of humour that it treats with desperate seriousness the funniest book of the age. The educated man who can read *Lady Chatterley's Lover* and not rock with laughter has a sick mind.

Let us return to the current superstition which sets such a high value on seriousness. It ought not to need saying that it may be the very seriousness of a book which makes it immoral. For the moral quality of a piece of literature is the extent to which it recommends moral as opposed to immoral behaviour. (Notice that it is not a question of whether it recommends moral behaviour, but whether it recommends moral *as opposed to immoral* behaviour. If a work of art recommends no particular kind of behaviour at all, it is not necessarily any the worse for that.) Immoral literature is literature which recommends immoral behaviour. If a play or a novel

98

wins sympathy for adulterers, sodomites, dope-addicts, or nymphomaniacs in the sense of making the audience or the reader feel that such people are right to indulge their vices and aberrations, then it is immoral. It goes without saying that a comic treatment of adultery or sodomy in a funny story or a bawdy piece of literature is most likely to be thoroughly moral; for the force of humour is frequently dependent upon stirring our sense of the incongruity between what people do and what they ought to do. Humour can rarely afford to dispense with the yardstick of traditional morality. Flippancy and wit may dispense with it—as we have seen in Restoration comedy and in Noel Coward—but not true humour. That is why Coward's allegedly comic work is, in the long run, so desperately unfunny. It stirs that terrible smile which is succeeded by sadness.

It is important not to give the wrong impression here. Obviously a play or a novel which deals with promiscuity or sexual deviation may win the audience's or reader's sympathy for the deviants in the sense of making them deeply aware of how easily one may be led into sin, sensitive to the appalling temptations that assail others, and correspondingly more penitently aware of their own weaknesses. It is possible to do all this in a work of art without for a moment implying that sin is other than sin, without in the least hinting that traditional morality needs to be amended to meet the modern situation. It is possible. But that it rarely happens is what one would naturally expect who has seen and reckoned with the drift of contemporary secularism away from the clarities of the Christian mind.

Enough has been said now, however, to indicate that over this issue the notions and vocabulary of week-end criticism relate to presuppositions which the Christian mind would reject. It is not the overt judgement of the critic that the Christian mind rejects ("This is a serious treatment of a real problem. It is a realistic picture of one of to-day's grim actualities. Utterly sincere, it has the authentic ring.") Rather it is the underlying assumptions that adjectives like *serious*, *realistic*, *sincere*, and *authentic* establish moral criteria superior to those of Christian ethics. When you are accused of trying to pervert the morals of the young by writing which recommends or condones vicious practices, it may be some excuse to claim that you were really only joking and that your tongue was in your cheek. It is no mitigation to argue that indeed you meant it seriously and in all sincerity.

We have now looked at two current notions which the Christian mind would reject. The one—a ready acceptance of divorce and remarriage as preserving the monogamous ideal—is gaining ground in society as a whole, but is especially strong among wealthy and well-to-do people, and may be regarded as a required conformity of the social establishment. The other—the assumption that any exploitation of sexuality in literature is justified by its seriousness—may be regarded as a required conformity of the new intelligentsia. Together they illustrate the need for the Christian to approach all social or intellectual groupings with a mind alert to the detection of error in their assumptions. In this sense the Christian mind is suspicious of fashionable conformities.

The increasing obsession with sexuality and vice in literature is defended to-day by an irrational and emotive exploitation of words like *sincere* and *authentic* which carry spurious "moral" overtones. The process of perverting language in order to glorify immorality has

100

gone to frightening lengths in some quarters. Perhaps an illustration of what extremists have already done in this direction will serve as a warning of what may lie in store should the present drift of "cultured" opinion continue unchecked. A recent edition of an American beat magazine, *Big Table*, published in Chicago, contains a series of articles by different hands celebrating the writer William S. Burroughs (author of *Junkie*, *Queer*, and *Naked Lunch*). Burroughs is a drug-addict, a self-confessed homosexual, promiscuous, and an alcoholic. This is how Paul Bowles describes life with Burroughs:

> His life had no visible organisation in it, but knowing he was an addictive type he had chosen that way of giving himself an automatic interior discipline which was far more rigorous than any he could have imposed on himself objectively.

And Alan Ansen writes thus of Burroughs's position *vis à vis* the "need for commitment".

> This commitment he finds in addiction to narcotics, an addiction which swallows up his income and gives him a new grim interest in the economy . . .
> W. S. Burroughs . . . a deeply committed personality. . . .
> He is an indispensable indication that it is possible to be vicious without being slack. How many addicts one knows incapable of more than a sob or a monosyllable, how many queers who seem to have no place in life except the perfume counter at Woolworth's or the economy price whore-house. To use drugs without losing consciousness or articulateness, to love boys without turning into a mindless drab is a form of heroism . . .
> Burroughs's attitude towards property is most austere.

I have quoted enough to show that in giving a bogus glamour to a life of vicious debauchery words like *interior discipline*, *rigorous*, *commitment*, *deeply committed*, *heroism*, and *austere* are employed in contexts which, to speak soberly, render them preposterous. The point to be stressed here is that this is only a further development of that perversion of language and concepts which is well begun in England already in the regular write-up of films, plays, and books, lowbrow and highbrow alike, in our daily and weekly journals. If the Christian mind does not sharpen itself to detect and expose what is bogus in moral attitudes and pronouncements at an early stage, one doubts whether any other force exists to check the disastrous drift towards the moral topsy-turvydom represented by *Big Table*. For the truth is, the Christian Church apart, there is no ethical tradition in our midst sufficiently rational and logical to withstand the assaults of modern immoralists.

A peculiar quality of the Christian mind is that, knowing the weakness of human nature, it expects conflict in the moral sphere. It assumes that the powers of evil will exploit every possible occasion for drawing men into the mental confusion of blurred concepts and twisted values. There is about the Christian mind a peculiar hardness—a refusal to be surprised at evil and depravity; an inability to be overcome by shock; an expectation that evil will be at large where God is not. Hence its cultivated suspiciousness of that which currently passes muster, in any powerful worldly circle, as the right thing. Hence, in the moral sphere, its zealous attention to the thin ends of wedges. It knows how evil grows.

It would however be dangerous to end this chapter at this particular point—the point at which one has forcefully stressed the Christian mind's full recognition of evil at large in the world, and even in the most respectable and exalted circles of it. It would be dangerous because there is so much more to be said. The Church comes with a judgement upon the modern world: but it is not the kind of judgement which enables the Christian to feel superior; not the kind which makes him say: "What a ghastly world this is that we Christians have to cope with" — not that at all. The Church's judgement upon the modern world is very different. It is properly expressed when we turn to our contemporaries and say: "Look what we've done, you and I; luxury here and famine there; juvenile delinquency, prostitution, alcoholism, the revival of slavery, racial discrimination; look what we've done. Look what our human nature produces when it gets a free hand, unrestrained by God. Do you want it like that? Do you like it? Is that your idea of a worth-while world?"

In other words, the Church would have us turn to the world in judgement, with the utmost clarity and power in our identification of evil, yet in full acceptance of our common guilt — and, finally, with a deeply moving message of hope. For the Christian mind cannot separate from its judgement upon the world and its judgement upon the self, its realization that the world and its inhabitants are nevertheless God's, by him created and by him redeemed. So we turn to modern man, as he stands at his council house gate or leans on his cocktail cabinet, and we say:

"Into just such a situation as this our Lord came. The world was rotten. Vice was rife. The wealthy lived in luxury: the poor were oppressed and down-trodden. There was debauchery and corruption in the cities of the Roman world as now in our own cities. There was slavery and injustice as in the darker parts of the world to-day. There was drunkenness and perversion. Bureaucracy prospered. Men bribed their way to power. There is no evil now which did not exist then, two thousand years ago. Nevertheless our Lord came. He came into the midst of it. And he found the shortage of residential accommodation so acute that he had to be born in a stable like the child of refugees or squatters. But he came, and he grew here, talked and taught here. He didn't come in style. He didn't wear an old school tie. He didn't flourish duplicated testimonials. He didn't have a good Oxford accent or an assurance bred of Public School conditioning. He came from a working-class home; he spoke a provincial dialect; and he had a body of followers some of whom might well have failed their eleven plus or their college entrance examination. He came here at the humblest level because, as God, that was where he wanted to be; where best he could work and serve and love. At the level of the factory-worker and the farm-worker, at the level of the under-privileged. He came. And he wasn't a great success in the world. He didn't have a brilliant career or climb the social ladder. He didn't acquire more and more prestige, status, and possessions. He didn't get on. He was more like you and me than like those expensively suited gentlemen in the glossy magazines who are surrounded by sleek cars, sleeker women, and smart furniture. He came, by every act and word to show up the world's evil, yet never to pretend it was not a world fit for him, the divine, to be in, and on the bottom floor."

If Christians think carefully and prayerfully, they will come to understand what the Incarnation means for them in terms of their twentieth-century vocation. They will learn at what points they can enter into enterprises and social groupings eagerly and at what points they must, conversely, probe, question, and withdraw. They will learn what are the proper twentieth-century modes of judging the world, of identifying the self with its sins, of being *in* and yet being *out* of this

104

world which our Lord inhabited and yet was not of. But these vital insights will be achieved only if there is among us a Christian mind sharp enough as an instrument of discrimination to cut cleanly through the befuddling mental jungle which constitutes the practical ethics of our secular society.

3

ITS CONCEPTION OF TRUTH

THE CONCEPTION of truth proper to the Christian mind is determined by the supernatural orientation of the Christian mind. When we Christians speak of "the great truths" of the Christian Faith, we mean especially those doctrines describing the meeting of the temporal and the eternal, doctrines testifying to a reality beyond our finite order, which has impinged upon that order and still impinges upon it; the doctrines of the Divine Creation, the Incarnation, the Redemption, the work of the Holy Spirit. To start with this illustration of how in practice we Christians use the word *truth* when we are thinking and speaking christianly is to indicate the full breadth of the chasm separating the Christian from the secular mind. For the Christian, truth is supernaturally grounded: it is not manufactured within nature. The violence of the collision between the secular mind and the Christian mind in this respect is often underestimated. One may say without exaggeration that failure to distinguish clearly between the Christian conception of truth and the conception of truth popularly cherished in the secular mind has been one of the most unfortunate neglects of our age. This failure has done more than anything else to sap the Church's intellectual morale. It has produced woolly sentimentality and evasion in the thinking of Christians themselves, destroying clarity and authority.

106

It has conversely nourished in the secular world the conviction that the Church has nothing to say to this generation deeper or more startling than the conventional platitudes of welfare ethics.

Briefly one may sum up the clash between the Christian mind and the secular mind thus. Secularism asserts the opinionated self as the only judge of truth. Christianity imposes the given divine revelation as the final touchstone of truth.

The marks of truth as christianly conceived, then, are: that it is supernaturally grounded, not developed within nature; that it is objective and not subjective; that it is a revelation and not a construction; that it is discovered by inquiry and not elected by a majority vote; that it is authoritative and not a matter of personal choice.

Ours is an age in which "conclusions" are arrived at by distributing questionnaires to a cross-section of the population or by holding a microphone before the lips of casually selected passers-by in the street. In many spheres of activity, quality is measured by mass-preference. The Top Ten or The Week's Best-Sellers indicate what is worth having in the way of new records or books. Listener Research gives marks to radio and T.V. shows on the basis of maximum audience-ratings. This deference to mass-preference of an admittedly capricious and non-rational nature is a phenomenon of the age. Educated people in general are wryly amused at this kind of thing: perhaps they ought to be more seriously concerned at the cumulative effect on the popular mind of the surrender of standards to the whims of the biggest crowd making the loudest noise. And perhaps they ought to be even more anxiously concerned about the status conferred nowadays on the opinions of the uneducated and the ill-informed.

This is a difficult and delicate topic to treat of. A right concern for quality and value can so easily be perverted into sheer snobbery. Nevertheless there are worrying aspects of the cult of the common man. The Primate makes a statement about public morals. It is based on the age-long teaching of the Church, well grounded in a profound understanding of man's nature. A popular London newspaper features the comments upon the Primate's statement elicited from a Chiswick typist, a Peckham butcher, a Billingsgate porter, and so on. The comments may well be replies to a glib question which does scant justice to the original subject of controversy. A bit of misrepresentation here, a bit of misunderstanding there, and a bit of tendentious reporting thrown in, and you have as the final product an unholy little hotchpotch of irrelevant illogicalities which provides five minutes of amusement for the educated reader, and useful fodder for the schoolmaster for his next discussion group.

But what is the effect upon the Chiswick typist, the Peckham butcher, and the Billingsgate porter? And upon all those who identify themselves with these as their fellows, their spokesmen? Surely the impression is conveyed that Christian teaching is open to veto by popular vote of all and sundry, however uninformed. The notion of a body of truth, solid, foursquare, behind the pronouncements of the ecclesiastics, is foreign alike to the questioner and the questioned. No one seems even to entertain the notion that there is a fabric of truth to be reckoned with in Christian Revelation if you challenge the derivative regulations for personal behaviour. The sense of an objective truth existing within the sphere of religion has been lost. Religious conviction is, for the secular mind, a matter of individual preference related, not to objective truth, but to personal need and predilection.

Nor is this a corruption of the popular mind only. It is perhaps equally prevalent among allegedly educated men and women. Some time ago an English bishop published a theological book which was reviewed by a well-known critic in one of the comparatively high-brow weeklies. The reviewer first summarized what the book was about, and then paid tribute to the clear way in which the bishop had expounded certain doctrines. Finally, however, she (it was a woman) added an astonishing observation to this effect: "But how un-necessary! Why can't Christians be good just for the sake of goodness itself, instead of having to drag God and all this theology into it?"

It would appear that this reviewer is so oblivious of the nature of Christian truth that she thinks the Chris-tian Faith is an instrument fashioned to serve a temporal end, namely the production of "good" human beings, by which she means men and women of moral integrity. In her eyes, apparently, the whole of our religious thought and practice is simply an elaborate device for improving ourselves as finite beings. She thinks the Christian's starting-point is this: "I'm determined to make myself a good chap, and I think Christianity is the thing to do the trick."

In an age and a country with a living Christian mind, this kind of thing would be greeted surely as one of the choice public howlers of the year. But we are so unused to thinking christianly that it is necessary to reiterate, even in Christian circles, that the Christian Faith is not a recipe for procuring goodness for ourselves as a desirable possession; that the Christian Faith is not a recipe for procuring anything. The idea that God's nature is studied, that God is worshipped, that the Church exists, in order to cultivate in men and women something called "goodness", as a nice and useful acquisition for their earthly career, reflects the reduction of the status of religion to that of a handmaid of secularism. As though we invented a God and constructed a theology as instruments for conveniently achieving something here below! If this were indeed the case, then Christianity would surely be a clumsy piece of machinery. One can think of less cumbersome ways of inculcating moral principles than that of constructing a doctrine of the Trinity and a doctrine of Redemption.

There is no subtler perversion of the Christian Faith than to treat it as a mere means to a worldly end, however admirable that end in itself may be. The Christian Faith is important because it is true. What it happens to achieve, in ourselves or in others, is another and, strictly speaking, secondary matter. For the Christian Faith will remain true whether we who profess it turn into heroic saints or into even more miserable sinners. We must insist that we worship God because he is God, not because we want something out of him. What a mean blasphemy it would be, to go through magnificent acts of public worship always with the dominant intention at the back of the mind — "This is really going to make a better chap of me!" What arrogance and presumption, to treat eternal God, throned in glory, as a visual aid to moral self-improvement.

To think christianly is to think in terms of Revelation. For the secularist, God and theology are the playthings of the mind. For the Christian, God is real, and Christian theology describes his truth revealed to us. For the secular mind, religion is essentially a matter of theory:

110

for the Christian mind, Christianity is a matter of acts and facts. The acts and facts which are the basis of our faith are recorded in the Bible. They have been interpreted and illuminated in the long history of the Church. The Christian mind is inescapably and unbrokenly conscious of the hard, factual quality of the Christian Faith. The Christian mind is alert to the solid, God-given, authoritative factualness of the Christian Faith and the Christian Church. Christianity has been called the most materialistic religion in history. That is an illuminating point. For Christianity is so much more than a mere moral code, a recipe for virtue, a system of comfortable idealistic thought. It is a religion of acts and facts. Its God is not an abstraction, but a Person — with a right arm and a voice. Its God has moved among us. *How wonderful are thy works!* That is a persistent biblical theme. Not, how interesting are thy theories. Not, how intense is thy being. Not even, how unanswerable are thy arguments. But, how wonderful are thy works. For Christianity is a religion of things that have happened — a Baby born in Bethlehem, a body nailed up on a cross. It is a religion of continuing daily action, centred around solid things like fonts and altars, bread and wine.

The secular mind will not have this. And, worse still, secularism has eaten away from the Christian mind that sense of Revelation's rocklike quality without which the Christian mind is no longer Christian. Hence the tendency in the modern world to treat the Christian Faith as though it were simply a series of interesting speculations, and Christian practice a matter of interesting experiments, all devised and made by men as part of their search for God and their pursuit of virtue. When secularism gives this debased status to the Christian

111

Faith, we have no cause to be surprised; but when professing Christians begin to accept the Christian Faith and the Christian Church at the valuation of secularism, then there is cause for alarm.

The popular modern unwillingness to reckon with the authoritative, God-given nature of the Christian Faith is bred of the anti-supernaturalist bias which dominates contemporary thinking, and is indeed native and natural to secularism. It is also nourished by the popular misconception of the nature of truth. Our culture is bedevilled by the it's-all-a-matter-of-opinion code. In the sphere of religious and moral thinking we are rapidly heading for a state of intellectual anarchy in which the difference between truth and falsehood will no longer be recognized. Indeed it would seem possible that the words *true* and *false* will eventually (and logically) be replaced by the words *likeable* and *dislikeable*. I have known educated people, professing Christians, who purposely gathered together for religious discussion men and women representing the widest possible varieties of religious conviction. This was fair enough. But unfortunately their aim, as they put it, was to get everyone to make his "individual contribution" (how fraught with error this phrase can be) so that collectively they might arrive at the truth. Now there is much to be said, socially and intellectually, for bringing together people of different outlooks and beliefs; but there is no rational basis for the notion that by mixing a number of conflicting views you are likely to arrive at the truth. You cannot construct truth from a mass of dissonant and disparate material. You cannot *construct* truth at all: you can only *discover* it. And the more noisily opinionated people intervene with their contributions, the less likely you are to discover it.

Yet, within the Church as well as outside it, this perverted notion persists. Truth is conceived on a quantitative basis—no doubt under the influence of statistical reasoning and public opinion polls. It is being assumed that the more people there are with different opinions to contribute, the greater "truth" will emerge from the mixing of these opinions in the melting-pot. Truth is regarded as a kind of pudding, or brew, which you concoct from human opinions. (This false notion of truth has done damage at some levels to the ecumenical movement.) But truth is more like a rock than a pudding—a rock which you lay bare by scraping away the soil. And the soil is largely compounded of human prejudice and passion.

Let us clear away a bit of soil here and now. Two opinions are rarely better than one. If A thinks rationally on a given matter and B thinks irrationally on the same matter, then neither A nor the world in general will benefit from having A's view adulterated with B's. Again, as someone wisely put it, if schoolboy X has got the right answer to a sum, and his eleven companions have got various wrong answers, then X would be a fool to compromise by accepting a figure averaged out from the twelve exercise books.

Christian truth is objective, four-square, unshakable. It is not built of men's opinions. It is not something fabricated either by scholars or by men in the street, still less something assembled from a million answers, Yes, No, and Don't know, obtained from a cross-section of the human race. Christian truth is something given, revealed, laid open to the eye of the patient, self-forgetful inquirer. You do not *make* the truth. You *reside* in the truth. A suitable image for truth would be that of a lighthouse lashed by the elemental fury of

113

undisciplined error. Those who have come to reside in the truth must stay there. It is not their business to go back into error for the purpose of joining their drowning fellows with the pretence that, inside or outside, the conditions are pretty much the same. It is their duty to draw others within the shelter of the truth. For truth is most certainly a shelter. And it is inviolable. If we start to dismantle it and give it away in bits to those outside, there will be nothing left to protect our own heads—and no refuge in which to receive the others, should they at length grow weary of error.

How, then, are we to reconstitute the Christian mind, so that we can deal with our contemporaries, outside and inside the Church, who fail to appreciate that the Faith we profess is something which has been given to the world from outside? For an erroneous estimate of Christian truth meets us almost every time we read newspaper comment on the Church or listen to religious discussion on the radio. All around us people speak of the Christian Faith as of something manufactured here, in this world, by human beings. It would be tedious to recapitulate much of the current nonsense, but it is necessary to give examples. Thus it is argued that Christianity makes too much of the after-life and not enough of this life; that Christianity does not cater properly for the weaknesses of human nature; that Christianity lays too much stress on sin; that Christianity is too dogmatic, exclusive, and bigoted.

Thus people talk. Why don't you bring your Christian teaching up to date? Why don't you get abreast of modern thought and scrap all this fanciful stuff about the Trinity and the Incarnation? Why don't you get rid of your outmoded belief in unscientific hypotheses like that of the coming of the Holy Spirit? Why not drop those impossible miracles from your teaching so that we can listen to what you have to tell us about living a good life?

Likewise there is criticism of the Church's rules and practices. It is argued that services should be brought up to date. Readings from the Old Testament might well be scrapped. Reading from the New Testament might fitly be supplemented or occasionally replaced by readings from Plato, Confucius, or Marcus Aurelius. The recitation of bloodthirsty psalms should be dropped. Healthy, upstanding men and women should abandon the morbid practice of proclaiming themselves miserable sinners. Thus the critics argue. There are men like Lord Altrincham who would gladly transform the Church into a humanistic ethical society devoid of creed and sacraments.

Now at this point I am not concerned to attack particular liberal or modernist notions as such. Rather I am concerned with the state of mind behind them—the presupposition on whose foundation all such controversies first arise. For undoubtedly the people who make these complaints about Christian belief and practice and tell us how to improve it, all reveal the same astonishing misconception—the idea that the Christian Faith is something which men have manufactured and which they have the right to alter; the idea that the Christian heritage consists of a code and a set of beliefs fabricated by human brains and therefore able to be altered or improved upon by human brains. Often the assumption appears to be that Christianity represents mankind's best shot so far at making a religion; that, if man had another try, he might do better next time.

When we come up against criticisms of the kind I

115

have illustrated, which treat the Christian Faith as something which needs to be reconsidered or adapted or improved upon, too many of us are inclined to reply in kind. We are seduced into defending this or that particular article of faith against the secularist mental background which presupposes it *alterable*. We slip naturally into the kind of reasoning which would be appropriate if the Christian Faith were a construction of the human brain—indeed the kind of argument which would be appropriate if the test of each and every article were its capacity immediately to satisfy individual taste and preference. Thus sometimes we find ourselves misguidedly defending by deductive argument what ought to be presented by historical affirmation. Now here is no attempt to disparage the use of reason in relation to matters of faith. Christians must always be prepared to display, as far as they are able, the rational quality of the Faith they profess. But we must beware of defending *primarily as theories* doctrines which are essentially descriptions of facts. For instance, it is useful, satisfying—and for many of us perhaps necessary—to appreciate the logical coherence and inevitability of the Virgin Birth within the framework of Christian theology; but we must never forget that the Virgin Birth is a fact, not a theory, that its validity is by no means dependent upon the tidiness with which it fits into our intellectual synthesis.

Were there a living Christian mind, the sense of the hard, factual objectivity of Christian doctrine would be widespread, and people would no more find themselves defending individually and in isolation the doctrine of the Virgin Birth than they would find themselves defending individually and in isolation the second law of thermodynamics. It is only within an essentially

116

secular field of discourse that individual Christians can find themselves illogically called upon to defend their attachment to particular doctrines as though they had personally devised or chosen these doctrines on the basis of private predilection. It is only within a liberal secularist society, dominated by the it's-all-a-matter-of-opinion code, that a street-corner orator or a knocker upon your door can assume it appropriate to pin upon you, as an individual Christian, the demand to defend this or that doctrine as though it were your personal possession—to explain your individual attachment to it as clearly and particularly as you would explain why you chose this wall-paper or that piece of furniture.

By allowing the Christian mind to be destroyed, we have imposed an intolerable burden upon ourselves as individual Christians. It is not surprising that so many shift the burden from their shoulders. We have accepted secularism's challenge to fight on secularist ground, with secularist weapons and secularist umpire, before a secularist audience and according to the secularist book of rules. Having done so, we look around in dismay at the discovery that our followers are few, our predicament misunderstood, our cause misrepresented. Hastily we try to plug the gap by pouring out more and more sermons and books of instruction "explaining" our cause, but doctored to the secularist mentality. It is high time to shift our ground.

My claim is that if we did shift our ground, if we set about reconstituting the Christian mind, and began by taking for granted the authoritative, God-given nature of the Christian Faith, and re-establishing in ourselves an unfaltering sense of the objectivity of Christian truth, we should find it an exhilarating procedure. So would our opponents. If they came with a complaint against the fantastic nature of a Christian doctrine or practice, then our first reaction would be to shake them out of the secularist assumption that that doctrine or practice is our personal possession or the product of our personal preference. "Look here," we should say, "I didn't invent Christianity. It wasn't made to *my* design. In fact there's quite a lot in it that I don't like at all—all this business about repentance and self-surrender, for instance. That stuff goes against the grain with me. But then, as I say, I didn't invent the Christian Faith. I just happen to believe it's true." Thus we must separate ourselves from our Faith and at the first stroke demolish the secularist notion that one can enter the Christian field of discourse dragging the it's-all-a-matter-of-opinion code at one's heels.

Secondly we must administer to the secularist mind a further jolt. "Look here," we add, "*no* human being invented the Christian Faith. It was God's idea. If you think it a bad idea, you'd better blame God. It's no good blaming me, or the rector, or the bishop, for the character of the Christian Faith. You'll have to blame God. He gave us this Christianity. We can accept it. We can reject it. But we can't tamper with it as though it were something put together by human hands or human brains."

Thus, to take another example, when the critic comes along and says, "Of course I believe in God, but I've no use for the Church. I can't see the need for it", then we are tempted to start arguing the case for the Church on the secularist presupposition that it is a human construction. We are led into arguing on theoretical grounds that the Church is a good thing because it brings people together, or that an organized institution is logically appropriate within the scheme of

118

salvation. And up to a point this may be a useful way of reasoning. But there is no doubt that, if we think christianly, we shall affirm the Church as a fact, and a divinely guaranteed one, before we defend its existence on logical grounds. We shall tell our critics that to talk of not seeing the need for a Church is to imply that Christians need not have bothered to have a Church; whereas of course Christians did not invent the Church: it is not something which they could either have had or not have had. We must not talk—and we must not allow critics of the Church to talk—as though the Apostles sat round a table in the early days and one of them said, "I propose we have a Church", and another said, "I second that", and it was carried *nem. con.* For the Church was not manufactured to a human plan. The Church happened. God made it, not man. He came to earth and left the Church behind him.

Therefore to talk of not seeing the need for the Church is like talking of not seeing the need for the moon. The Church, like the moon, is not a human project, but a divine creation. It is before us. God put it there. Speculators might argue that, in his omniscience and wisdom, God might have thought up some different instrument of salvation, just as he might have devised a different means of lightening our darkness at night. But where does that kind of speculation get us? We are not concerned with what God did not do: we are concerned with what he did. And one of the things he did was to come to earth and establish the Church.

The Christian mind has an overriding sense that the truth it clings to is supernaturally grounded, revealed not manufactured, imposed not chosen, authoritative, objective, and irresistible. If the Christian comes before the secular mind claiming less for Christian truth than is its due, he not only betrays the Faith, he contributes to the erosion of the Christian mind. The Christian Faith has to be defended for the right reason. Too long we have been defending it for the wrong reason, trying to win a place for it in secular esteem by claiming that it ministers to ends served by secular welfare, and that it can be turned into a personal philosophy adequate to give solace to a secular mentality through a secularist career. We have to insist that the Christian Faith is something solider, harder, and tougher than even Christians like to think. Christianity is not a nice comforting story that we make up as we go along, accommodating the demands of a harsh earthly reality with the solace of a cherished reverie. It is not a cosy day-dream manufactured by each person more or less to suit his own taste. It is a matter of hard fact. We Christians appreciate its hardness just as much as those outside the Church. We are as fully aware of its difficulties as the outsiders are. We know that, in a sense, Christianity leaves us with an awful lot to swallow. No Christian, thinking christianly, divesting himself of the easy self-deceptions of secularist thinking, will pretend that Christianity is an easy faith—easy to accept, easy to explore, easy to rest in, easy to explain. It isn't. We must outdo the unbelievers in agreeing with them on that subject. We must stand at their side and look with them at this thing, the Christian Faith, and vie with them in detaching ourselves from it. "You find it difficult? So do I. You find it awkward? So do I. You find it unattractive? That's exactly how I often find it myself, especially round about 7 o'clock on a Sunday morning. You think it a thundering nuisance? In a way I quite agree with you. It *is* a nuisance at times, especially in Lent. But it's *true*, you know."

That's the point. It's true. The Christian mind is alive, quivering with the awareness that here is truth and all truth. Nourished within the culture of a Christian mind, the individual Christian shakes off that outrageous, secularly imposed notion that Christianity is his, something he is desperately and earnestly responsible for, the product of his subjective election and the expression of his personal predilection, like his new tie or his latest L.P. disc. Nourished on a vital Christian mind, we should no longer face with such acute discomfort the glib taunts of a blinkered secularism: "But surely you don't dig angels and things like that! I say; do you allow them wings and nightdresses? ... But surely you wouldn't tie together for life a man and a woman who have come to hate each other! Would you have them copulate like beasts, loathing the sight of each other's face? Is that what you mean by Christian marriage? I'd no idea you approved of that sort of thing. I imagined you'd find it quite repulsive. . . ."

In reply we shake the fetters off: "My dear fellow, I'm not responsible for the Church. I'm not the author of the creeds. I didn't devise Christian ethics. I didn't map out the Church's doctrines. So don't ask me what I like or what I approve of. Ask me what I think is *true*. The truth isn't always nice. It isn't always likeable. But I believe you've got to cling to it."

That first. There is need for much reasoning later. But the reasoning must be carried on within a Christian field of discourse. And until the foundations of a hedonistic secularist individualism have been at least shaken, it is doubtful whether anything useful can be said.

The thesis of this book is that the chances that the Christian mind will shake the foundations of secularist

121

individualism are not very great at a time when secularism has all but shaken the Christian mind to pieces. Even some of what passes for Christian apologetic is nowadays dominated by secularist thinking. We have all come across those intensely well-meaning books in which intellectuals describe their long, long search after a faith to live by among the numerous creeds and philosophies which have appeared during man's history, and their eventual arrival—almost reluctant arrival, it seems sometimes—at the decision that there is much to be said for Christianity after all. These books have titles like *Man's Quest for God, My Search for a Creed, Adventure after Faith, Journey to the Truth*, and so on. In them academic figures explain how, toilsomely through ten or twenty years of reflection and study, they have won through to a belief in the reality of spirit, or the immortality of the human soul, or the existence of a transcendent and beneficent deity. These are men who in middle life arrive at a position of some intellectual comfort—the knowledge that our cherished western values are after all worth something, that Christian morality is a great bulwark against savagery, and that the best thing to do is to accept as much of the accompanying dogma as one can swallow. The more adventurous of these writers tell their readers that they have investigated the various religions and philosophies of history, that they all point vaguely in the same direction, but that Christianity is by and large the best brand of monotheism on the market.

It would be wrong to dwell derisively on sincere strivings after truth. But, in all charity, the Christian must note the unhealthy aspect of any long-term policy of studying your way to God at the fireside by means of library books. We must deprecate the idea that God has been so unjust as to locate himself at the end of a long course of academic study which you wouldn't be equal to if you failed your eleven plus or your college entrance examination, and which you wouldn't have time for if you contracted galloping consumption. It is dangerous to suggest that arrival at God's truth can be attained only after years of study needing a trained academic mind. God is not so unloving, so unjust, as to have weighted faith in favour of the intellectuals. The spiritually robust man does not need to plough through even one volume of Gifford Lectures before he can confidently recite the Apostles' Creed.

But here and now it is more relevant to stress another and graver objection to the view of religion taken and presented by these patient searchers after truth. That is, the dangerous emphasis their attitude lays upon the individual man's formulation of his beliefs; their failure, even at the end of their recorded pilgrimage, to sense the hard, objective given-ness of the Christian Revelation—that overbearing, authoritative factuality which in the long run makes the constructions of any individual mind petty and irrelevant. These apologists carry their secularist presuppositions with them to the end, finally trying to embrace and contain within an individual frame of reference that blinding fabric of truth which could dazzle the brain of an Augustine or an Aquinas. That is why books of this kind are so often saddening to read: because they testify to the appalling difficulty of trying to teach the modern intellectual to think christianly.

After all, if the Christian Faith is true, we are not in the kind of world in which men have to grope their private way to truth through utter darkness. It is far simpler than that. We do not need to clutch desperately at a bit of evidence here and another bit of evidence there until we have gathered together the material from which a working creed can be fabricated. God is not so cruel as to have left us in the miserable plight that the most saving and necessary truths have to be laboriously assembled by everyone for himself. We are not a lot of amateur detectives on the hunt for clues in a cosmic whodunit. That is not the world as the Christian sees it. For that would be an abandoned world, a world on which God had virtually turned his back—a world in darkness from which God's light had been withdrawn. Men have need to fabricate neither their creed, nor their moral code, nor their picture of the purpose of the universe. God chose not to leave his world in darkness. He chose to lay open in it the revelation of himself. That is what Christianity is all about. All pseudo-Christian poses which deny, ignore, or diminish this truth are grounded in this-worldly prejudice in favour of human self-sufficiency. In short they express a fundamentally secularist outlook. Over against it, the Christian mind reiterates that the Christian Faith is not a human fabrication but a divine gift. When people encounter the Church and her message, they do not come up against the opinions of men; they come up against the word of God.

The current failure to distinguish clearly between matters of fact and matters of opinion is of course a feature of contemporary intellectual life in general. No one who listens to the professional questioners and their victims on radio or television can be unaware of this confusion. That it should have infected thinking within the religious field is not therefore surprising. In failing to draw a sharp line between those questions which are left to ourselves to decide upon, and those which are inevitably settled for us by the very nature of the Christian Faith itself, we succumb to a besetting error of the age.

The drift of secular culture in this respect is clear enough. There is a revolt against authority in favour of popularity, against quality in favour of quantity, against value in favour of magnitude. No one is more sadly aware of this than those who work in the field of education. If numbers of candidates fail an examination, it is no longer assumed that the candidates are at fault; it is suspected that the examination is at fault. That an examination should serve the purpose of rigorously sifting candidates of intellect or industry from those who are unintelligent or lazy is a notion now outmoded. An examination is expected to provide a qualifying label for those who sit it. If some candidates fail it, the complaint is heard that public money has been wasted in educating these candidates and in running the examination for them. It is a small step from this to imply that an examiner who fails an examinee is therefore in that act guilty of wasting public money.

We who work in English education know of men who have resigned from lucrative examinerships rather than continue further to contribute to the lowering of our standards. In many examinations final pass levels are determined by statisticians, who insist that in the final graph the curve shall be what it always has been. In short the "normal" proportion of entrants must pass, irrespectively of how much standards in general may have slipped. And this kind of thinking has corrupted universities as well as schools. It will be observed that the most celebrated men in the educational world are those who are prepared to display their learning by translating unpalatable but plain propositions like,

125

"We must lower our university standards", into congenial slogans like, "We must cut out the wastage of university students".

This illustration from the field of education is intended to reflect a prevailing drift of our culture. Men are less prepared than they were to stub their toes against unpalatable objective truth, to measure their littleness against high objective values, to discipline themselves for a test of strength in a rigorous objective examination. This is because a secular tradition has now fully established itself which teaches that man's fulfilment and success lie, not in screwing himself up to the demands of a high vocation, but in moulding all that he encounters in service to his needs. As long as man's destiny is seen in terms of mastery, we shall suffer from this debased tradition. For the coin of mastery, whose good face shows us painstaking scientists harnessing the natural order in the service of human needs, has a bad face too, which shows us the modern mass mind demanding, not only food that can be easily eaten and entertainment that can be easily enjoyed, but also examinations that can be easily passed and status that can be easily won.

Were there a living Christian mind, encountered at every point as the thinking of our age hammers itself out in conversation, discussion group, lecture room, radio interview, and private study, then the situation would be more hopeful: for young men and women everywhere would find their easy assumptions bruised against the sharp edges of a rocklike tradition. But we look for the Christian mind in those places where it ought to be forcefully, even harshly evident, and we find not a rock but a bog. From the cosy clerical studies and the sunlit closes the secularist voices, thinly disguised, drone on. "A number of modern theologians are of the opinion that ... More and more thinkers in the Churches are coming round to the view that ... Up-to-date scholarship is beginning to hold that ... Post-Bultmann insights serve to remind us that ..." Who would think that Christian theology is a solid, objective body of knowledge, in its essentials fixed and unchangeable? It is made to appear like a collection of capricious conjectures or majority opinions which change with the fluctuations of intellectual fashion. The notion that Christian teaching is in a state of perpetual flux, the notion that Christian truth has to be adapted to the needs of post-Freudian man, these are not at bottom otherwise rooted than the notion that examination papers have to be adapted to the capacities of post-war youth. All these delusions spring from the erosion of objectivity. All in different ways testify to human abdication at the rational level. They are in tune with the growing assumption that all questions of belief, morality, and value, are matters of opinion as capricious and individual as one's personal taste in socks or radio comedians.

Yet there are those in the pulpit who, instead of asking, "What is the teaching of the Church on this point?" ask, "What do the latest modern theologians have to say about this point?" For the slavery to fashion always takes over when the discipline of objective truth is removed. (Just as, in the choice of furniture or clothes, the slavery to fashion takes over when the discipline of objective value is removed.) The latest becomes as important in the pulpit as it is in the salon or the boudoir. A Bultmann comes in here: a Dior comes in there. I wish I too could believe this comparison as unjust as many of my readers will pronounce it. Unfortunately it is assumed that God rates human scholars in an order of preference based upon inverted chronology. It is a strange delusion that God, in disseminating wisdom and illumination to theologians, automatically awards the highest prizes to those whose temporal births are the remotest from his own.

In this connection it is unfortunately true that those whose sense of objectivity is weakest tend to be correspondingly most assertive in expressing their opinions. Logically and psychologically it seems to follow that subjectively opinionated people are those whose opinions are most individualistic. If one is conscious of drawing one's convictions from a solid, deep-rooted tradition, one inevitably has a sense of quiet assurance in one's beliefs and a feeling that is the reverse of touchy defensiveness. If, on the other hand, one is bursting with notions which gush from sheer personal predilection operative outside the discipline of any tested tradition, one will naturally have a strong urge to advertise and justify them. In other words, it is off-centre thinkers who tend to draw attention to themselves. Within the Church this has especially unfortunate consequences. A man whose sense of intellectual discipline is weak may thereby be unable to recognize and respond to the coherence, the all-of-a-pieceness of the Christian Faith. This same weak sense of intellectual discipline makes him unregulated and self-assertive in his thinking generally. In other words, failure to appreciate the objective fabric of Christian truth for what it is—as something quite independent of he-say and she-say and personal idiosyncrasy—this failure occurs most notably in subjectively opinionated people who are weak in self-discipline and deficient in self-knowledge. In the religious sphere self-knowledge throws the

128

intellect prostrate before the immense authoritativeness of Christian orthodoxy; and the force of habitual self-discipline bends the will in obedience to the power behind the Church's doctrinal formulations.

Thus it will always be the unsound clergy who seek most to draw attention to themselves and to get a large public hearing. Heresy is itself a form of undisciplined self-assertion. That assertiveness, where it is strong, will emerge in other ways too.

A tragic aspect of all this is that outsiders think of the noisy rebellious heretics as representative of the Church. The public hear fallacious deviations from orthodoxy uttered by clergy in the Press or on the air, and imagine that theirs is the Church's teaching. Off-centre clergy often acquire neatly devised techniques of passing themselves off as being in the swim or in the know. "Of course the best Anglican scholarship to-day would hold that . . . Of course most up-to-date Christian thinkers have come round to the view that . . ." The effect of gambits like these, unsubtle as they may appear to the cunning mind, can be potent on the untrained mind. Some of the insidious implications they convey are worth analysing. One is the pernicious notion that, in theology, amendments are continually being made by a kind of democratic committee procedure carried out among a lot of learned men (whom you and I would scarcely be able to understand, but with whom the speaker by good fortune happens to be on familiar terms). Another false implication is that established Christian truth is more or less non-existent. There is only a mass of individual opinions, which sometimes agree together in sufficient numbers to produce a probable proposition.

Because adherents of this atomized and anarchistic

thinking often shelter under a spurious academic prestige, it is necessary to handle them roughly in controversy.

We have now said enough to show how contemporary secularism, heavily biased as it is towards individualism, subjectivism, and atomistic intellectualism, is quickly eroding what remains of the Christian mind. For the Christian mind is orientated towards a truth revealed, demanding, and divinely guaranteed, whose objective certitude and authoritativeness are alike distasteful to a secularism deeply committed to self-culture as opposed to self-discipline, and to a destiny of mastery as opposed to rigorous service. The push-button is an apt symbol of our age. It can be operated from an arm-chair.

But the tragic keynote of our age is atomism. It is nuclear fission which has destroyed our hope and our security, and threatens to destroy our civilization and our species. It is likewise the atomistic philosophy of Wittgenstein and his successors which has destroyed healthy philosophical thinking in our universities and which threatens to destroy philosophy itself. It is too the atomism of anarchic individualism which has destroyed the cohesive forces that ought to discipline our social, cultural, and national life. And it is the atomism of departmental thinking which has brought about the disintegration of human study and experience into separate unrelated compartments.

In tune with the numerous drifts towards fission is that anarchistic atomism in the intellectual field which is destroying man's awareness of, and responsiveness to, objective truth, and substituting a reliance upon personal predilection and collective opinion that is rooted in individualism. The theological aspect of this atomism is that it represents the dismemberment of man. The physical corollary which this spiritual and intellectual disintegration alike seem to point to is the atomization of the world we live in. The idea that nuclear annihilation might come, not as a cataclysm cutting off the natural development of our civilization, but as the logical culmination of its present drift, is too painful to be dwelt upon; but it is not too outrageous to be mentioned.

4

ITS ACCEPTANCE OF AUTHORITY

BY THE very nature of the Christian Faith, as
hitherto represented in this book, the Christian
mind has an attitude to authority which modern
secularism cannot even understand, let alone tolerate.
It follows from all that has been said about the God-
given nature of the Christian revelation and the
Christian Church that they must command a whole-
hearted allegiance from Christians; for Christians are,
by definition, men who accept the revelation and the
Church for what they are, the visible vehicles of God's
action in the world. That which is divinely established
and divinely guaranteed calls forth from men, not an
egalitarian attachment, but a bending submission. One
cannot seriously contemplate the first elementary truths
of Christianity—the doctrine of the divine creation of
man and his world, the doctrine of the Redemption, and
the doctrine of the Church, without realizing that here
is something which is either authoritative and binding
or false; deserving of submission or of total neglect.
Reason allows no place for a casual, one-man-to-
another approach to God and his demands. It is either
the bowed head or the turned back.

It follows equally from all that has been said about
the doctrines of individualism and self-sufficiency
permeating current secularism that our age is in revolt
against the very notions of authority that are crucial to

Christian thinking and acting. That there is a *good* element in contemporary rejection of authority is not to be denied. There is of course a strong admixture of good in most of those ideas which do damage to the minds and lives of men. Thus the modern rejection of authority in the West is closely associated in most people's minds with the overthrow of Hitler and Mussolini, the struggle against totalitarianism everywhere, the opposition to Soviet communism, the fight against imperialism and against the oppression of subject races, the defence of freedom of utterance, the resistance to power-grasping bureaucracy, the struggle against increasing standardization, and in short the protection of freedom in all departments of life.

Indeed the current rejection of authority is so intimately bound up in people's minds with the worthwhile and noble efforts of our generation that one is staggered at the magnitude of the task of trying to rehabilitate the concept of authority as something estimable.

It may be that there are a few aspects of our civilization to which we can point with some hope of winning sympathy for the notion of authority—the law, for instance, or perhaps even, after the shocks of the last decade, the hierarchical structure which gives age control over youth and teachers control over pupils. But for the most part we move in a world in which thinking and feeling alike are coloured with a distaste for authority unparalleled in history.

This is true, for instance, of the authority of the State. It is ironical that respect for the State's authority seems to have been greater in ages when the State operated tyrannically and unjustly than now, when it is for large numbers of people a benevolent agency. In

133

spite of (or because of?) pension books, family allowance books, and other provisions of social welfare, the modern mind does not sense the authority of the State as benign and estimable.

Rather it is seen as something faintly ridiculous and unworthy. And modern man is not wholly wrong about this. Consider the matter existentially. Ask yourself under what visible shape the authority of the State impinges upon the life of the average citizen from day to day. What is its concrete manifestation? There is to-night, perhaps, a voice on the radio saying things in the name of the government. (They are all, to the last minute detail, entirely *expected* things: otherwise they could not be said. No listener is the wiser for having heard them.) But to-morrow night another voice, with comparable political and intellectual credentials but representative of a rival party, will come to assert that these things said to-night are utter nonsense, complete fabrications, a travesty of the truth, that the policy they represent can lead only to the ruin of the nation. Meaningless mutual contradiction at the highest political level is not conducive to respect for authority. (This is not to deny that it may have a most healthy aspect, considered in relation to other practical matters.)

Then, representing the State at another level, there is that bored-looking man behind a grille in the post office, who nonchalantly pushes at you a family allowance, an old-age pension, or a wireless licence. He does it with the same air of weary and sheltered aloofness with which the railway clerk aims at you the very cheapest of cheap half-day returns. His mien seems to imply that he himself never has need of these mundane things to prop up his comfortable existence. Then again, of course, there are the forms to be filled in, a

134

standing joke for redundancy and ineptitude. These are the things which bring the State's authority immediately and concretely before the eyes of modern man. Is it surprising that they make a poor impression? If we voice our secret thoughts, they represent something rather shabby and unworthy, something of which in our better moments we are slightly ashamed—that suave, platitude-laden voice on the radio, that weary-looking official behind the grille, that ill-devised collection of words on the paper so inferior. These things represent something which, we inwardly feel, deserves to be circumvented by a man of spirit. The men who govern and administer the State, at any level, are now felt to be part of a machine; not free agents, but involuntary links in a vast mechanism. "They're only doing their job", men say, nodding in superior sympathy, as the police tackle a criminal, or a cabinet minister churns it out from the front bench. Of course. For we cannot regard our cabinet ministers as men with wills and convictions of their own. We know they cannot afford the luxury of being thus human. They take the party line when they speak. They have no choice but to speak thus or to get out. Modern man tolerantly indulges them in their limitations as he indulges a pet dog. It can't reply rationally. It can only bark. Poor thing. It does its best. In an endeavour to show that it too exists—though on a lower level of perception and sensitivity—it wags its tail. What else can it do?

It is symptomatic of the general development of our society that our political leaders have accepted relegation to a sub-human level of existence at which they function as parts of a machine. In their political capacity they cannot operate humanly—let alone christianly—for they cannot exercise the human prerogatives of

135

reason, choice, decision. It is doubtful whether the cabinet minister has more freedom functionally than the worker at the mass-production line. Philosophers who have studied the dehumanization of man in modern society have hitherto neglected this abdication of humanity which a political career imposes upon a man to-day. If you continue at all times to exist humanly — that is to say, thinking and acting by reference to principle, reason, and purpose — then you automatically and inevitably bring about your expulsion from political life. That there is no room for human beings — still less for Christians — in modern politics is something which thinking men have now accepted at the back of their minds, though they have not fully faced the fact at the conscious level.

In the context of the wholesale, and not unjustified, denigration of authority by the secular mind, one has to reassert christianly the principle of authority. First, God's authority; then the authority of his revelation, his commandments, and his Church. And here, right at the start, one encounters a new difficulty. For the task of re-establishing the notion of God's authority is obstructed not only by the current depreciation of authority itself but also by a false, pre-established picture of God — found even within the Church. Certainly the Church has preserved the concept of a loving God, a merciful God, a compassionate God. But have Christians generally themselves any vivid sense of God's power and his dominion? Do we, when we worship God or when we reflect upon his nature, catch a clear echo of his resounding and indomitable majesty? Are we inwardly and vitally aware of that tremendousness before which all the greatest achievements of human civilization shrink to insignificance? It cannot

136

be denied that this is the God we are supposed to worship—not just a companionable God who is to be sidled up to and nestled against, but an awesome God before whom the worshipper prostrates himself, a wrathful God whose raised right arm can shake the universe.

So far is modern man from thinking christianly that he has the acutest difficulty in trying to combine together in his mind the two vital concepts which we have just united in our picture of God—the concept of love and the concept of power-laden authority. As a result of historical developments and changes of psychological habit the idea of authority has been totally severed from the idea of love. There is an iron curtain between them. They now belong to two different modes of thinking. Yet it was not always so. There was a time when these two key concepts were blended together in the embracing idea of Fatherhood, which has provided the richest summing-up of God's significance for us. The father was the loving provider and defender whose hand was open in liberality and raised in protection: he was also, at the very same time, the awesome ruler to whom implicit obedience was due. But in the modern world notions of supreme authority are not involved in the connotation of fatherhood. There is now something faintly ridiculous about the idea of a father trying to assert binding authority in the home. Yet God remains, in religious utterance, pre-eminently our Father, even though a father, as currently imaged, is no longer either authoritative or even dignified. For the comic strips in the cheap Press have reduced the father to the stature of a genial and clumsy butt. He is a friendly but rather awkward bear about the house. He fills up the armchair, he has to be kept in a good humour; but he must not be taken too seriously. He

137

is a little obtuse, in a half-winning, half-wearing way. In reposeful moments he can be the best of company: at awkward moments he fumbles and exasperates. He is the poor fish who pays for unauthorized purchases by wilful and frivolous womenfolk. He loses his pipe, forgets his umbrella, drops parcels in the street, and bursts the buttons from his braces. His highest delights are provided by the sporting pages of the daily Press; his familiar misfortune is the lawn-mower; his bitterest agonies are associated with income tax.

This image of the father is reproduced here in order to indicate the extent to which, in current thinking, the lovable has become the very antithesis of the powerful, the loving of the authoritative. One must see it as part of a deep and comprehensive rebellion of the modern mind that concepts involving love and lovableness should be shorn of connotations hinting at authority or power; while concepts involving authority and power should be shorn of connotations hinting at love or lovableness.

There is much in modern life that continually deepens the separation between the idea of authority on the one hand and ideas of what is loving and lovable, awesome and inspiring, productive of devotion and deserving of respect. Consider under what forms the average man meets closely with *personal* authority. In most cases probably under the form, firstly of the headmaster, and secondly of the employer. These are two familiar symbols of authority for the common man in the modern world. The headmaster's authority is often for a time awesome. Perhaps it is the most fearsome and *mysterious* authority that modern man generally encounters in the course of his life. But the great thing about it is that one grows out of it. It is revealed, in the long run, to have been after all a bit of a fraud. That awesome potentate, once so mighty and terrifying, was he after all nothing more than this frail, wizened, pathetic old man with the asthma and the rheumatism, who couldn't hurt a fly? The dominant authority encountered in childhood turns out to adult eyes to have been as hollow as a dream. One can laugh now; but it hurt once. In plain words, the whole thing was a frame-up. The mighty authority was a sham imposed upon childish credulity.

As for that other personal symbol of authority, the employer, thanks to increasing progress in the world, he has had his wings clipped. Men look sideways at their bosses as they drive out of the works in their cars. They can afford to raise their eyebrows knowingly as the car sweeps by. The boss is no longer dangerous. They have got him taped. There was a time, before the unions got the upper hand, when the boss was a menace. He'd be a menace again if men grew careless of their rights or weakened their togetherness against him. In short, employers are rather like wild animals, at present safely caged by the unions and by the watchful legislation of a politically egalitarian state. Men have got the measure of their bosses. Collective pressure keeps their power within limits. To keep their claws cut is progress.

Thus authority looks in the modern world to modern man. That is its face and the reaction it provokes. Authority is something whose grip you grow out of, something you break away from. It is something you view with suspicion, something you combine against in order to limit its operations. How far does this kind of thinking colour man's conception of God and his attitude to the Church with its claim to spiritual authority? How far is modern man, by the very nature

139

of his upbringing and his mental inheritance, rendered almost incapable of conceiving divine Fatherhood, benign yet authoritative, loving yet powerful, merciful yet wrathful? There is no doubt that, in reconstituting the Christian mind, an early necessity is to purge the concept of authority of its shabby and sinister undertones. And it is scarcely necessary to point out that secularism's low estimate of authority has infected thinking within the Church, so that many of those whose duty it is to rehabilitate the notion of authority are busily occupied in further discrediting it. For in this respect secularism's attack upon the Christian mind is an emotively powerful one, and Churchmen readily succumb to it. By an easy, but false, transference, the democratic rejection of tyranny and privilege in the political and social set-up is metamorphosed into an anarchic rejection of intellectual, moral, and spiritual authority within the Christian Church.

We have already seen how secularism's it's-all-a-matter-of-opinion code has been applied indiscriminately over fields of thought and experience where instructed judgement ought to prevail. This code is inimical to the Christian conception of truth and the Christian conception of authority alike. Secularism's publicity merchants have an insidious method of bringing this code to bear upon matters of faith and morals to which it can never properly apply. When a bishop makes a pronouncement about some topical question of belief or behaviour, the journalists contrive to present it to the public as though it were merely the individual bishop's personal opinion. Of course bishops do sometimes speak their minds on matters which are for each man to decide for himself — matters of economic policy which are at issue between the two parties, for instance. Quite naturally Churchmen do not find themselves all in agreement on matters of this kind.

But unfortunately secular organs of publicity manage to put across episcopal statements of an authoritative doctrinal or moral nature with the same flavour of that's-his-private-opinion which accompanies statements of a more personal character. Thus, for instance, when the Archbishop of Canterbury voices the Church's age-long ruling about divorce and remarriage, or about euthanasia, the secular publicists manage to give these statements the flavour of personal opinions. The impression conveyed is that His Grace has just reached a most difficult decision after long weighing the pros and cons. A vague feeling is left in the air that another bishop, or perhaps the next Primate, might have other views.

What the secular mind is ill-equipped to grasp is that the Christian Faith leaves Christians with no choice at all on many matters of this kind. The Archbishop of Canterbury has no more freedom than you or I to decide christianly in favour of divorce. That is so by the very nature of the Catholic Faith as received by the Church of England. There is no such thing as a body of opinion against remarriage and a comparable opinion in favour of remarriage. There is only understanding of the Christian Faith on the one hand and ignorance of it on the other. There is only obedience and disobedience.

The same may be said about episcopal pronouncements on the subject of artificial insemination by donor. The secular press heralds and reports these pronouncements as though they represented interesting individual contributions to a debate which has only just opened, which will continue for a long time, and will in fact never reach a conclusion. But, so far as the Church is concerned, there is no debate. There *can* be no debate —

except with the world. For the Church has certain established doctrines guaranteed by the word of God himself. It is by reference to these fundamental doctrines that spokesmen for the Church pass judgement upon moral questions which are being publicly discussed.

It is no more possible for an informed and disciplined Churchman to speak in support of A.I.D. than it would be for a loyal communist to praise the capitalist system. Both hypotheses are self-contradictory absurdities. If a "loyal communist" praised the capitalist system, in so doing he would cease to be a loyal communist. If an "informed and disciplined Churchman" condoned A.I.D. or remarriage after divorce, in so doing he would cease to be an informed and disciplined Churchman. There is nothing to argue about here. Indeed, christianly speaking, there are fewer vital things in life to argue about than we fondly imagine. God is not the unjust deity we would make him out to be. He does not make attainment of his truth dependent upon your having a good brain, a flair for argument, and the time to keep abreast of all the latest contributions to theological or moral controversy.

In this connection one must deplore a familiar trick by which spokesmen of the secular world manage to pass off authoritative truth as individual opinion. I mean the habit of referring to Church dignitaries by their personal names instead of by their proper titles. For many years we heard far too much, in print and on the air, about "Dr Fisher" and far too little about "His Grace the Archbishop of Canterbury". The headline which ought to have read "The Church and Divorce" frequently read "Dr Fisher on Divorce". The damage done by this under-the-belt attack upon the Church's authority is more serious than has been appreciated. The propaganda value of pinning "opinions" on persons, which are in fact authoritative truths or regulations, is considerable. The practice lowers the currency of doctrine. It depresses episcopal authority. It cheapens the Church's status. Above all, it secularizes the mind.

For the Church carries the institutional authority of a Body established by God and guaranteed by our Lord as his own Body, the vehicle of his continuing life in time. The Church carries the intellectual authority of a truth given to men in divine revelation, warranted and witnessed to in miracle and martyrdom. And the Church carries the moral authority of a way of life divinely ordered and involving defined disciplines and practices. Moreover the Church carries the spiritual authority of a divinely granted commission to heal and teach, to baptize and forgive, to bless and eat the bread and wine.

The Christian mind, aware of all this, is dominated by a demand for submission and obedience. The Christian mind conceives the Christian fact as something which claims, possesses, controls, and overpowers. Over against this, the secular mind conceives the Christian fact as something to be claimed or not claimed, to be possessed or not possessed. And in so far as the individual mentally claims Christianity instead of being claimed by it, mentally possesses Christianity instead of being possessed by it, he has failed to shake off the secular presuppositions which debar him from thinking christianly. In short, one may think secularly about the Christian fact in the very act of proclaiming oneself a convert.

This, to revert to the subject of the last chapter, is the position of the intellectual who arrives at Christianity by eventually picking it up as the most worth-while thing on the philosophy-of-life stall. Fortunately, of course, men who reach this stage may go through it to another, very different one. The purpose of this book is not to judge men, whatever their religious position, but to clarify a problem by defining states of mind. We are not directly concerned with moral culpability or even here with exhortation. The question whether it is better to be a Christian incapable yet of thinking christianly, or an unbeliever, is obviously irrelevant to us. This needs to be said to clear the air, for it is now necessary to add that many people first begin to approach the Christian Faith with a mental attitude wholly or largely secular in its operations. Thus a man may recognize the need to posit a God behind the universe because otherwise he finds the origin and purpose of life inexplicable. Having posited a God, he may go further and persuade himself that Jesus Christ comes nearest to representing what divinity must be like.

Tenuous intellectual admissions of this kind often no doubt lead to something solider and more nourishing. As they stand, they represent a state of mind far removed from the Christian. A God is posited because the brain likes it like that: it wants to dwell upon a cause as well as upon an effect, upon a purpose as well as upon an activity. In other words, the individual intellect summons up a God in order to satisfy its thirst for system and order. Man's intellect wants a complete picture of the shape and meaning of things, and it proves artistically desirable to insert a God in the top right-hand corner of the composition.

It is important not to denigrate the demands of the human intellect. The Christian believes that God has given us our reasoning powers: we haven't manufactured them ourselves. Nevertheless it is equally important not to miss the sharp distinction between an intellectual demand for a God to fill up a humanly composed picture, and the Christian's awakening to the fact of a divine revelation in time by which an institution, a book, a tradition are presented to him charged with the weight of an absolute and transcendent authority. A mere intellectual demand for a God to fill up the picture is essentially secularist in spirit and in motive, in that it claims a God only to enrich and complete a finite situation. But the Christian's awakening to the fact of divine revelation serves to shatter the apparent completeness of the finite and to impoverish human experience in so far as it has been confined by that delusive "completeness". Moreover a mere intellectual demand for a God to fill up the picture is secularist also in the sense that it is rooted in the human urge to mastery. The metaphysical free play of the human mind by which God is docketed along with absolute values, moral imperatives, and the like, is itself as secularist in spirit and purpose as the manufacture of rockets with a view to reaching the moon. In so far as twentieth-century activities are grounded in the spirit of human self-sufficiency and directed towards the establishment of human mastery over the universe, they are equally remote in themselves from christianly directed activities rooted in the sense of human creatureliness.

This is not to deny, of course, that both metaphysical speculation and space research can be carried on within the synthesis of christianly directed thinking and practice. Our purpose here is simply to clarify a crucial distinction: that between claiming the Christian God as a useful intellectual convenience or acquiring the Christian Faith as a satisfying intellectual possession—

145

and awakening to the tremendousness of a God-given revelation in time. The key to the difference may be said to lie in the word *authority*. For it is the binding authority and authoritativeness of the Christian Faith which, holding the Christian mind in its grip, puts that mind in the reverse situation from that of the secular mind trying to hold the Christian Faith in its grip. The one state of mind leads to that sense of personal inadequacy, human dependence, utter lowliness and lostness, which brings the Christian to his knees and throws him into the hands of our Lord. The other state of mind leads to a case-hardened self-satisfaction of the pharisaical kind with which our Lord himself never came to terms.

It is important never to confuse the notion in the head that a God probably exists with the motion of the will that flings a man on his mercy. Here is perhaps one of the Church's hardest tasks in the pseudo-Christian climate of our country to-day. It has to deal with people who are quite ready to admit that there may be a God, but who have never felt the slightest impulse to abase themselves before him. There are men and women who feel positively virtuous in having mentally allowed for a God in the scheme of things. One may well ask how the Church can stir them to that sense of dependence, creatureliness, gratitude, and unworthiness, without which, christianly considered, their pretence to reckon with God is a mockery—a living rebellion. For the Christian God is something much more than the author of the answer-book to that volume of problems we call "The Mystery of Life". God is not the bolsterer of our human wisdom, the buttress of our self-sufficiency. He is the despoiler of our human self-reliance. His Name does not head the list of contributors to the fund for extending our empire of mastery; rather his Signature seals the death-warrant of our egotism.

Thus the intellectual who arrives at the position of declaring that "Jesus Christ comes nearest to representing what divinity must be like" is a long, long way from Christian self-commitment. His declaration represents an authoritative judgement upon our Lord—while the Christian's position is that of accepting our Lord's authoritative judgement upon himself. The blasphemy implicit in this reversal of rôles makes one pause. A declaration in which the human brain sums up our Lord as from a superior position is surely wholly secularist in its rejection of divine authority. To *place* our Lord, to speak words which presuppose that the human being uttering them is in a position to know *a priori* what divinity ought to be like, and to evaluate our Lord's claim to have approximated to this ideal, this is, christianly considered, topsy-turvy. One pictures a competition in which entrants compete for the title of "the Divinest Person in History", or else perhaps "King Universe", and the judges' panel awards highest marks to Jesus of Nazareth. No doubt it is better to give first prize to our Lord than to give it to Lenin or Hitler or Aleister Crowley, no doubt it is always better to approve of our Lord than to disapprove of him; but all these attitudes, christianly considered, are fraught with pride. Of course, in studying a particular declaration here, one does not attribute to the speaker personally the degree of presumption which, if analysed, his statement might be said to express. We are rarely as bad as the worst things we say, and never as good as the best things we say. Besides we have been conditioned by our own upbringing in a society in which, as our thesis proclaims, there is no living Christian mind. It

147

inevitably follows that when a man reflects christianly on current attitudes and scrutinizes them rigorously in the light of Christian presuppositions, he shocks others—and himself. The shock is inevitable as one discovers, by logical process, the extent to which pseudo-Christian poses have sprouted and flourished in an environment lacking the discipline of a rigorously operative Christian mind.

Anyone who has been trained to think christianly holds the authority of the Church always at the back of his mind. Because his contemporaries generally think secularly, even when discussing religion, he finds himself separated from them by an apparently unbridgeable gulf when the talk turns to the subject of the Church and the modern world. Thus some of the most common slogans of men inside and outside the Church jar against the first presuppositions of the man who thinks christianly. "The Church must adapt itself to the modern world", one says. The Christian thinker reels; then fumbles. He is first dizzy with the shower of "buts" that fly into his brain, then dazed with the sheer difficulty of sorting the confusion out. There is a limited, specialized sense in which it is true that the Church must adapt itself to the modern world. But over a whole range of controversial issues—and in the deepest and most controversial sense—it is rather true that, far from the Church adapting itself to the modern world, the modern world must adapt itself to the Church. In short the slogan accepted at every other conference or discussion as an unquestionable axiom is a preposterous falsehood. For if the Christian faith is true, and the Christian Church the authoritative vehicle of salvation in time, then it is the most urgent, inescapable need of the modern world to adapt itself to the Church.

What are we Christians about, if not that? What is our Father's business, if not that?—namely, the task of bringing the modern world into the Church—of adapting the modern world at every point in its social moral, and political life, to the demands of the Church.

The virtual disappearance of the Christian mind from the contemporary scene means that whenever discussion arises about the Church, it is carried on against the background of a prejudice which is never brought to light, but which may be defined as favouring the *Authority of the World*. One finds the Church not only attacked on the wrong grounds, but also defended on the wrong grounds, as ministering healthily to the well-being of a temporal set-up. Secular criteria of well-being are established, and then the Church is judged for its success in measuring up to them. A controversy may be carried on between men attacking the Church and men defending the Church—and yet the two ostensibly hostile parties may be deeply united in a mental secularism from which a christianly trained mind would recoil. How often does this situation arise in the modern world? Is it an exaggeration to claim that it has become the familiar dilemma of the Christian trained to think christianly? He is urged to commit himself in relation to a controversy overtly representing the struggle of Christianity with unbelief, yet he recognizes in the undertones of both contestants a fundamental respect for the authority of the World which sharply cuts him off from sympathy with either.

"The Church must move with the times," it has been said; "otherwise it cannot serve as an effective instrument of human progress." The Christian thinker reels again. Yes . . . but . . . but . . . but . . .

First of all, since the newest thing is not necessarily

149

the best thing, it is not automatically and inevitably good to be up to date. Secondly, since the Church is the vehicle of eternal life and eternal truth, it is superior to all "times": it is of the Church's essence to represent an unchanging and timeless reality in a changing, time-locked world. Modern man is the victim of an incurable, self-imposed slavery to ephemeral fashion. How then can he savour the full quality of a message and a way of life whose character it is to be substantially the same in A.D. 300 and in 1963?

Then, *ought* the Church to serve as an instrument of human progress? If that means progress in faith, in grace, in godliness, no doubt it should. But if some other kind of progress is in mind—that progress in welfare of which the politicians talk so much—then the answer is, Yes and No. The Church has its own work to do, and it is always concerned with human welfare; but its notion of human welfare is not secularism's notion by any means. Pre-eminent in the Church's concern for a man's welfare is its interest in saving his soul. When people talk about human progress, they are not generally thinking of progress towards salvation. But that is the kind of progress which matters primarily to the Church.

In the background, more profound and comprehensive than these fallacies, is the pervading, brooding notion that the Church is a means of achieving something secularly worth while, something which secularism can measure and approve. In short, here is the heresy of the authority of the World. Half the misguided and misleading chatter about the rôle of the Church to-day goes astray on this point: it conceives of the Church as a means of achieving something rather as, say, a car is a means of getting from London to Edinburgh. But the

Church is unique and indispensable where the car is not. If you haven't a car, you can take a train to Edinburgh, or you can fly. And in the days before cars and trains and planes people went by ship, by horse, or by coach. Even now there is nothing to stop you from riding on horseback to Edinburgh, or from walking there if you have time. Now the Church is not a means of achieving something in the sense that, if we got tired of it and dispensed with it, we could find some other means of doing the same thing, serving the same end. It is not at all a means than which some other might conceivably be found.

A more apt image would be to see the Church—in relation to eternal life—as like an orchestra in relation to a symphony. The symphony exists in the composer's mind and on paper, an abstraction and a printer's diagram. There is only one thing in the whole world which can make the symphony real for men and women—an actuality of their concrete experience—and that is an orchestra. If no orchestra is available, it is useless to present the composer with a sewing machine or a vacuum cleaner. Both are excellent instruments, and each is capable of producing a not wholly unpleasing sound, but on neither can you perform a symphony. So far as human experience in general is concerned, no orchestra means no symphony. And the Church likewise is the only vehicle of eternal life in time. It is the Body of Christ on earth. Men and women are at liberty to become members of it or to detach themselves from it. But they are not at liberty to suggest that it be changed into something else. There is nothing else to change it into. For, like the orchestra, it fulfils its purpose only by being exactly what it is. Of course you can improve the Church's members as you can rehearse the

151

orchestral players to a greater proficiency. It is fair enough to ask them to tune up. But it is one thing to tune up a harp, and a very different thing to get rid of the harp and substitute a draining-board.

The doctrine of the Authority of the World has bitten deeply into the thinking of Christians to-day. Professing Christians will rise to baits which they ought never to touch. They will write articles in the Press, or give talks on the radio, whose central thesis or starting-point is deeply rooted in secularist presuppositions. We have had more than one series of articles recently on "The Church's Desperate Crisis". One has seen it proclaimed that the Church is facing its "gravest crisis for centuries". The Press delights in these topics. "Can the Church Survive?" "Is Religion on the Way Out?" "Is there a Place for the Church in the Modern World?"

Were it not so tragic, surely it would be laughable that a world poised on the brink of an H-bomb war should have time to ask, "Can the Church survive?" Can the Church survive, indeed! Can the *world* survive? As for the Church's desperate crisis; if a desperate crisis is something which puts the very existence of an institution in jeopardy, then the Church is certainly not facing one. The world is. No doubt of that. But the Church can never be destroyed. It cannot even be gravely damaged. It cannot be decimated numerically: too many of the Church's members are already beyond the barrier of death; too much of the Church is already safe home. It is perhaps the case that we—twentieth-century Christians—are the last few millions to live on earth in membership of the Church. Perhaps the end is to be soon. What then? Has not an enormous, immeasurable concourse gone before? No doubt we have reason to feel ourselves to-day a frail, straggling, unheroic Chris-

152

tian band. But look at the tremendous men and women we follow! It could be, in the eyes of God, that the twentieth century's contribution to the universal Christian Body is the sorriest and least distinguished of all. It *could* be so. Personally, I don't think it is; but it is a possibility that has to be allowed for. If it were indeed the case, it would be understandable that our Lord should have chosen to put the heroes at the front and the feeble laggards at the back.

But whatever the quality of twentieth-century Christians, the Church remains unalterably secure. And no Christian who understands the Church's true nature can talk of the Church as being in danger of being engulfed. It is too late for the world to destroy the Church, two thousand years too late. The world had its chance and did its best—and its worst—on Calvary. God answered with a body of men and women against whom the gates of Hell shall not prevail. We have his word for it. And if the gates of Hell shall not prevail, need we worry unduly about the latest secularist estimate of the Church's statistical manpower or the jibes of shallow brains-trust intellectuals who have yet to find their peace?

The world is like a great express train hurtling towards disaster—perhaps towards total destruction. And in this truly desperate situation certain passengers are running up and down the corridors announcing to each other that the Church is in great danger! The irony of it would be laughable if it were not so searing. Why, most of the Church's members have already got out at stations *en route*. And we ourselves shall be getting out soon anyway. And if the crash comes and the world is burnt to ashes, then the only thing that will survive the disaster will of course be the Church.

153

"The Church's Desperate Crisis." "Will the Church Survive?" "Can the Church Rise to the Needs of the Modern World?" Headlines like these may disturb or intrigue the minds of readers, Christian or non-Christian, who have swallowed the doctrine of the Authority of the World. But no one who is deeply rooted in the doctrine of the Authority of the Church can take them too worryingly to heart in the sense intended. For the Christian's image of the Church is that of a mighty liner in mid-ocean riding out a storm. Safely on deck, one cannot take seriously the cries of those who, having jumped overboard into the perilous sea, scorn the proffered life-belts, and use up their last resources of energy before being engulfed to warn those still aboard that they are in a doomed vessel.

The error of picturing the Church as a fading or dying institution has its converse too. Just as pessimism about the future of the Church represents a secularist habit of measuring in terms of the World's own criteria, so too the wrong kind of optimism about the Church's future here below may reflect a comparable deference to the Authority of the World. In this connection there is a phrase in current use among Christians which seems to epitomize the disappearance of the Christian mind. I mean the phrase "The coming great Church". It is an imprecise phrase packed with misleading undertones. It seems to suggest that experiments in Church-making have been faulty and scrappy as yet, but that eventually the real thing will emerge. It seems to imply that there is something truer, sounder than anything we have yet known in the way of a Church, which will shortly be discovered. It hints that the Church's true "greatness" lies in the future. Yet the Christian, thinking christianly, accepts that we *might* be near the end of

154

history, and that therefore most of the Church might lie behind us, and that there might be very little of it yet to come. We do not know. In any case, the Church is God's creation, and it is improper to speak of it as primarily and essentially a human project in the making. Above all, we must not transfer from the secular to the religious sphere the fallacious nineteenth-century doctrine of progress. We Christians are not engaged in laying the foundations of an institution, still less in improving an evolving or developing institution. We are engaged in being built by our Lord into his mystical Body, already unblemished, and needing no future to make it "great". The Church, thank God, is not coming. It is here, and has been here for a very long time. We fall into abject submission to the Authority of the World if we talk as though the real thing, the thing that could fully and absolutely command our allegiance, were yet to be manufactured, yet to be established. No Christian, thinking christianly, will ever speak of the Church as something which is yet to "come", still less as something which is yet to be made "great".

Enough has now been said to indicate how deeply secularist thinking has eaten into the Christian mind in this respect, destroying the Christian's overriding awareness of the supreme authority of the Christian Faith and the Christian Church, substituting for it a subtle and furtive commitment to the view that even a supernaturally grounded institution may legitimately be attacked or defended by reference to presuppositions which are basically antithetical to its very existence.

5

ITS CONCERN FOR THE PERSON

CHRISTIAN THINKING is incarnational. The Christian mind surveys the human scene under the illumination of the fact that God became man, taking upon himself our nature, and thereby exalting that nature for all time and for eternity. Thus the Christian's conception of the human person is a high one, his sense of the sacredness of human personality being deeply grounded in revealed theological truth. The status of the personal is such, in Christian eyes, that it ought not, for instance, to be subordinated to the mechanical.

It is a platitude to say that we live in the age of the machine. Technological mastery of the material world by mechanical means is the key to progress as modern secularism conceives it. Servitude to the machine is a mark of contemporary worldliness, and as such is a challenge to the Christian mind. This servitude has two aspects—the practical aspect and the theoretical aspect. The practical aspect is the fact that modern man is increasingly living his day-to-day life in servitude to mechanical contrivances. The theoretical aspect is the fact that the machine has now produced a way of thinking as well as a way of living. That way of thinking has its influence quite outside those spheres of life to which mechanical things are relevant.

No argument is needed to prove that modern men

frequently live in practical servitude to machinery. We all know men and women who take out their cars instead of walking two hundred yards to the post-box or the tobacconist's. There are men and women who not only drive themselves everywhere they have to go but also drive their children wherever they have to go too. The evil results of this particular servitude to the machine are well known. Human beings are deprived of beneficial exercise. Human beings in many parts of the world are prevented from having a healthy human relationship to the natural environment by the press of traffic and the fumes of petrol and oil.

In some parts of the U.S.A. this problem has reached sensational proportions. One has heard of mothers who not only drive their daughters to and from school four times a day, but also spend four or five evenings a week driving them to and from music lessons, dancing classes, dramatic clubs, youth meetings, and the like. An American mother explained to me once that she was inevitably a half-time chauffeuse until her daughter should be old enough to have the ignition keys flung at her in relief. I have myself had an experience in Detroit which will strike English readers as bizarre. At eight o'clock one evening, looking for the Ford Auditorium where a symphony concert was to be held, I found myself, in the middle of this vast industrial city, unable to contact anyone who could tell me the way. There were skyscrapers and brilliant lights all around me on the great roads flanked with bright shop windows. The cars flowed by, as usual, in their thousands. But the wide pavements were deserted. In no direction could I see a single pedestrian. It was some ten minutes before I found one.

This experience may have been, to some extent, the

157

product of coincidence. But the eerie loneliness of personal solitude in the midst of crowded urban civilization, shrieking with lights and roaring with traffic, struck me as a commentary on the drift of our increasingly mechanical and mechanistic culture. No doubt it is in Detroit, the heart of the world's automobile industry, that one would expect to find the effect of the car on contemporary civilization most vividly 1epresented. But it would be foolish to pretend that the drift of things is any different in our own cities. It would be a mistake too to judge the inhabitants of the U.S.A. as somehow more corrupted than ourselves by the automobile. An English visitor to the U.S. is inevitably impressed by the vast distances which have to be covered by many citizens in the ordinary course of their lives. The very lay-out of cities and their amenities presupposes the use of cars. We in this country who try to impose the same pattern of automobile-dependence upon our choked and congested little market towns, even though we mostly live within walking distance of shops and friends, have small cause to flatter ourselves that we are less committed in soul to mechanization than are the Americans.

A diabolical feature of dependence upon the car is that it increases in a vicious spiral. *Because* all the "respectable" people are in cars, it has become unsafe to walk, at least after dark, in certain areas of American cities. *Because* the car is used excessively and driven too fast, it is unsafe to allow a child to walk to school in many areas. The ironical stage has been reached at which cars are being used to protect children from the dangers of cars. Nor is this ironical development restricted to cars. Every intelligent parent is aware that it is the mechanical inventions designed to make life

158

easier and to dispel worry, which have made the care of children a more onerous and worrying business than it once was. Let any mother picture a situation in which there are no motor vehicles in the streets outside her house, no gas taps inside, no electric points, no gadgets. In this situation one would worry a good deal less about the whereabouts of young children from moment to moment.

This, however, is something of a digression. For here is no intention to depreciate the value of mechanical contrivances which minister helpfully to the satisfaction of truly human needs. Our concern is with the abuse of mechanical contrivances by men and women who succumb to their influence and allow their lives to be dominated by them. The car provides one example, television another, radio a third, and the cinema a fourth. Excessive use of these contrivances reduces man's life to a sub-human level, replacing choice, decision, and purposeful activity by a drugged acceptance, a mindless inertia.

Yet where is the Christian comment upon this crucial development in contemporary life? No doubt there is plenty of humanistic criticism of the mechanistic drift of our civilization, but one looks in vain here as elsewhere for the illumination of Christian thinking. Yet the doctrine of the divine creation of man, together with the doctrine of the Incarnation, establishes a conception of the human status more exalted than any other. Men are made in the image of God. Our humanity has been assumed and redeemed and exalted by our Lord himself. We know, as Christians, that our calling is to live as free, choosing, active men and women, making the best use possible of a world which is God's creation too. Truly Christian comment upon the human situation

159

would warn us against exploiting our world in the mere pursuit of comfort and ease, against allowing our God-given faculties to atrophy through inertia, against submitting ourselves in abject slavery to the material products of other men's brains and muscles, products which ought to be used in disciplined service of God and our fellows.

The notion of self-respect needs to be rethought by the Christian mind. We need to consider very carefully how far we are being dehumanized by contrivances which, properly used, can serve truly human ends in the highest degree. We have to ask ourselves what degree of dependence upon the technological artefacts that are drugging the bodies and minds of our contemporaries is appropriate in those who are trying to live the Christian life.

It is relevant to mention at this point that the mechanical gadgets of modern life, brought before the minds of men and women as they are by the most forceful and insidious resources of propaganda, minister gravely to covetousness and vanity, and to worldliness in general. No one who is in touch with contemporary attitudes, in suburbia especially, can be unaware of this danger inherent in the production, distribution, and advertisement of contrivances like cars, television sets, refrigerators, telephones, radiograms, electric washers, spin-driers, and so on. There is a prevalent conception of the good life which is based primarily upon possession of these contrivances. Men's notions of what the good life is—that is to say, what things are to be desired as constituting the fullness of life, and how these things are to be obtained—are frequently centred upon acquisition and enjoyment of these contrivances. Taken together, their successive acquisition provides a ladder

160

of progress in life which becomes one's purpose in living. This purpose can dominate the mind to the exclusion of more unselfish and less materialistic aspirations. It is ironical that, at a time when moralists lament the decay of the family as an institution and the cheapening of family life, the home should come into its own as a centre of significance in a novel and perverted fashion. For to the purchase of successive gadgets designed to improve the home and the family's diversions men devote themselves with great zeal and perseverance. The ladder of progress through an increasing number of such purchases—telly, fridge, washer, record-player, spin-drier, phone, car, motor-mower, etc.—provides an incentive for labour and earning which often precludes wider and more generous ambitions. The ladder can in fact give a meaning to life which is terribly complete and final. It may exhaust for modern man the meaning of daily work, so that higher purposes are swallowed up in striving to satisfy the ever-increasing demands of modern home life.

Thus, for those who strive, and for many too who have not the perseverance to strive, the possession of these contrivances becomes representative of what the full life means. It would be idle to close our eyes to this fact: that the fullness of living, as it appears in the prevailing secular vision, is the daily use and enjoyment of the maximum number of gadgets and contrivances that technological science can provide.

It follows that the diverse influences which feed the delusive passion of this new materialism ought to be everywhere under fire from articulate Christians nourished on a Christian mind. Men who amass fortunes by the exploitation of this passion have a lot to answer for. That the majority of men and women are not so intelligent as their exploiters is one of the keys to modern corruption. Our civilization is still based on a tension between the exploiters and the exploited, even though it is no longer true that the exploiters are the inheritors of vast wealth and the exploited their poverty-stricken victims. Nowadays the exploiters are the inheritors of intelligence and the exploited their less mentally gifted victims. Whether this represents a worse evil than the more purely economic injustices of last century is a matter for dispute. The relevant point here is that comparatively intelligent men are reducing fellow-human beings, children of God called to be inheritors of the kingdom of Heaven, to the status of mindless creatures scrabbling furiously after bundles of coils and cog-wheels packaged in chromium plate, their appetites stimulated and whetted by the lure of explicit and implicit advertisement in all the publicity devices of the day. Artists, psychologists, technicians, all prostitute their talents to this end, though it is big business as ever that makes the big money.

And where is the Christian mind, feeding its stream of prophetic judgement into this situation? Where are the priests and prelates pointing the finger of condemnation at the men — or, if they dare not, at the system — which thus dehumanizes modern man? Can it be that *all* the exploiters are Friends of the Cathedral?

It is perhaps necessary to forestall a possible misunderstanding at this point. The question of modern man's dependence upon the machine has been confused for us by the familiar antithesis between mechanized life and life in accordance with Nature. Since the nineteenth-century Romantic Movement, many thinkers and poets have lamented man's increasing dependence upon the machine, contrasting the life of modern industrialized society with an idealized version of pastoral life, idyllic in its simplicity and innocence. As a result of this antithesis it is too readily assumed that a thinker who dwells on the dangers of increasing mechanization is himself advocating a movement back to Nature. But of course the Christian's concern over mechanization does not derive from any dreamy illusions about natural man's innocence. The familiar antithesis between mechanization and Nature largely misses the point. We do not lament the increasing dependence upon mechanical contrivances because it removes man from the natural, but because it removes man from the supernatural. That is to say, mechanization, abused as it is, seduces man from the service of God to a life of servitude to material possessions.

Servitude to machinery has bred not only a way of living but also a way of thinking. The dependence upon machinery and the attention given to machinery have influenced men's habits of thought so that the machine has been accepted as a pattern of significance applicable quite outside the realm of the technological, applicable even to the domain of human relationships. Thus, in its most comprehensive form, this kind of thinking produces theories of the universe and of life which are frankly called "mechanistic". But the fruits of the machine's influence on the human mind can be seen in assumptions much less comprehensive and less articulate than any specific philosophy. They can be seen in popular assumptions about the nature of human societies and communities, and about the way in which the human brain and the human will should grapple with the affairs of life.

We tend to see ourselves as born to function in a series of mechanisms. We are born into an economic machine, a political machine, and a social machine. The secular idiom of the day uses the words *machine* and *machinery* freely in relation to diverse kinds of organization, social, financial, cultural, and so on. We even hear of the "educational machine". Talk of administrative machinery teaches us to view our home city as a machine within the larger national machine, incorporating economic and social mechanisms which are parts of a larger and more complex whole. Journalists and politicians do not allow us to forget that economic, productive, and distributive mechanisms involve us every day of our lives, while the mechanisms of national and local administration reach out to embroil us at every opportunity. These mechanisms are rightly so called in that they claim us, not as living persons, but as creatures of function. In relation to the production machine I am significant only as a unit of labour; in relation to the political machine I am significant only as a personified vote; in relation to the mechanism of distribution my functions are to devour food, to burn coal, to wear out clothes; in relation to the various administrative mechanisms I function, in turn, as a householder, a rate-payer, the driver of a car, the earner of an income, and the owner of a hose-pipe with one nozzle.

It has been suggested that men can be so engrossed in performing functions in contemporary society that they have neither the time nor the energy left for the business of merely being human. Certainly one must admit that it can be an engrossing business to operate successively as a solicitor, a viewer, an informed voter, a car-driver, a householder, a tax-payer, a rate-payer, a consumer, a dog-owner, a unit in Listener Research, and a stand-by for the Gallup Poll. One might consider this list as representing a full-time assignment with a variety of interests calculated to exhaust the positive resources of the mind and the will. It is a healthy achievement of the more positive existentialist philosophers that they have shown us contemporary man as an uncomfortable compound of multitudinous functions all too rarely integrated around a living existential centre. Powerful influences of government and commerce nourish the concept of man as a packet of diverse functions. There is lavish expenditure on numerous devices which appeal to man as the creature of one function only—propaganda, advertisement, entertainment, and indoctrination designed wholly to capture the undiscerning eye and the unthinking heart of man the conditioned consumer, the conditioned voter, the conditioned producer. Every effort is made to debase man by dehumanizing him; to condemn him to an existence in which he functions, not as a person, but as a thing; not as a thinking, choosing, creature, but as a cog in a piece of machinery. To function in a machine is to function sub-humanly — to act in a preordained, automatic pattern which precludes the exercise of purpose, creativeness, choice, and reason.

The extent to which mechanistic thinking is corrupting our culture might be illustrated in relation to any number of fields of activity. For instance, our educational system suffers disastrously from the dominion of the administrative mind, which is, by the very nature of modern administration, generally mechanistic in its thinking (and therefore unfitted to overlook strictly human affairs). It is a well-worn, but none the less just, joke among teachers that education is now a minor by-product of local authority administration. Classroom work is overlooked by superfluous local organizers. A county's schools will be run from the authority's central

165

office rather as a ring of chain-stores is run from head-quarters. As the grip of the administrator tightens, the authority and influence of the teacher and headmaster are correspondingly reduced. The headmaster is increasingly prevented from regarding himself as the leader of a vital community of persons. The telephone stands on his desk to remind him that, like the manager of a branch-store, he is in charge of one among a net-work of mechanisms operated from headquarters. The headmaster, who ought to be the link between school and parents, is now the link between the school and the local authority's offices. The wheel has come full circle. Men of personal conviction, with vision and purpose, are often considered too "dangerous" to be appointed to headships. Some appointing authorities seek "safe", mediocre men who will sit meekly at the far end of the telephone wire and do what they are told.

This illustration of the growth of mechanistic thinking in the world of education is particularly relevant because it shows in more advanced form a brand of corruption which is also eating into the life of the Church. The Christian mind, with its exalted concep-tion of the human status, recoils from any thought or practice which debases that status. The Christian will think in terms of persons and institutions; but modern secularism thinks in terms of units and mechanisms. The mechanistic mind conceives of the school as a mechanism without an existential centre: it has lost the concept of the school as an institution. The antithesis between an institution and a mechanism is an important one. An institution is a fellowship of persons united by community of purpose. A mechanism is an assembly of parts linked by interrelatedness of function. Purpose belongs to persons, function to things. Function is

166

enslavement to an automatic process governed from without. Purpose is the expression of the living personal will. Function is the activity of the object: purpose is the activity of the subject. Inspiring leadership can mould the sympathetic purposes of individual persons into a common pattern of activity, potent and harmonious. This is not machinery: it is life. But personal leadership is something which an elaborate administrative machine, by its very nature, can only destroy.

It is scarcely necessary to say that the supreme archetype of the living institution as opposed to the dead mechanism is the Church. The Church is the pattern of all institutions. It stands as one in unity by the power of an indwelling Spirit. I do not know whether historically the concept of an institution existed before the establishment of the Christian Church; but there is no doubt that in the Christian era all concepts of human societies bound together by a common spirit have taken to themselves something of the essential quality which belongs supremely to the Church.

How far has the debilitation of the Christian mind resulted in the spread of mechanistic thinking about the Church within the Church? This is a question which disturbs many who consider the proliferation of committees and administrative mechanisms under the wing and direction of Church Assembly and modern diocesan administration. There are no doubt some who would proclaim the very existence of Church Assembly as itself evidence of an improper intrusion of secularism into the life of the Church. Without going as far as that, one can at least point to the ever-present danger that an organizational network which can only be called "administrative machinery" will in fact function as machinery, and in so doing will exert a strong pull

167

towards enslaving or debasing men rather than serving their high purposes.

We have already pointed to the dangerous development of appointing men to the episcopacy on the grounds of their alleged administrative experience and ability. The thinking behind such appointments is mechanistic. If the concepts of personality and purpose are submerged under those of function in bringing men into the stream of the Apostolic Succession, then indeed the authority of the World has triumphed over the Church, and the living institution has been treated as a dead mechanism. There is food for grave thought here. It is in just such particular instances of surrender to secularist thinking that the Christian mind is gradually pummelled into unconsciousness. It would be difficult to think of a more pernicious and wholesale perversion of Christian thinking than that which, in elevating a man to an episcopal throne, would obliterate the concept of the shepherd and his flock, and substitute that of the well-oiled functionary required to operate a series of mechanisms from headquarters, as one might run a string of stores. From the concept of the overseer it is a small step to that of the machine-minder. From the concept of the machine-minder it is a small step to that of the big-end which swings the crankshaft. In so far as one allows mechanistic thinking to seep upwards from the life of manufacture and commerce to that of society, and then to that of the Church, one reverses the Christian mission, which is to cause Christian thinking to flow downwards from the life of the Church to that of society, and then to that of commerce and manufacture.

The case of the appointment of bishops is important because it is topical, and because of the key position of bishops in the Church as an institution. The very notion of episcopacy, if it is not corrupted, precludes the conversion of the Church into a machine. Every appointment of a new bishop ought to be such that it will remind us of the Church's true nature, not such that it will encourage us further to ignore it. Too many influences operate to that end already. There is much in the day-to-day chatter of committees, conferences, and Church journalism, which expresses a way of thinking subtly infected with a mechanistic bias. One reads such generalizations as the following:

> It was agreed that the industrial field is the largest and most important area of national life on which the Church is at present making little impact. Urgent measures are needed to rectify this defect.

When men talk like this, willy-nilly they give the impression that there is some other way of spreading the Christian gospel than the slow personal process by which the priest or the layman brings the Church's witness to bear upon Mr X or Mrs Y. That "other way" is never defined, but in the back of the mind there resides a hazy notion that it exists as some form of nebulous impersonal mechanism. You only need some organizational change, some administrative readjustment, some alteration in technique, some redeployment of resources, and this quick, efficient, unspecified mechanism for spreading the gospel can be brought into play.

This is the kind of delusion fostered by much loose thinking and speaking to-day. There is talk of "the Church" making "an impact" on the industrial field, and straightaway one tends to picture a large-scale advance by the forces of Christendom which, by comparison, dwarfs the laborious gains made week by week in the

169

parishes. One is seduced into conceiving of a sudden change in the machinery of evangelism by which a massive network of new contacts is built up, linking vast numbers of factory workers with an imaginary administrative centre where priests sit at desks with telephones in their hands. To speak thus loosely of rectifying a defect inevitably lures the modern mind to think of settling an irksome deficiency of power by popping in new sparking plugs that bring the old car up to full strength, or inserting a new fuse-wire which floods the old house with light again. It is becoming dangerous, as well as inappropriate, even to hint at mechanistic patterns of thought in speaking of Church life. In a sense problems are made to seem too easy, and the age-old disciplines of the spiritual and pastoral life become irrelevant, if the Church is conceived as a machine. For you can always alter or adjust the mass-production machinery so as to produce a wider curve in the car bodies here and a sharper corner there, to produce more red in the finished cloth here and less green there. But you cannot manipulate the Church's machinery so as to produce a bit more Christianity here in the industrial field. We are beginning to set up an educational assembly line so efficient that, by tampering with the machinery, we can produce a few more physicists here and a few more secretaries there, a few more primary teachers for the Midlands in 1966 and a few more contented machine-minders for the South in 1968; but we have not yet turned the Church over to an assembly-line system.

In this connection one must deplore the increasing tendency in the Church to talk of directing evangelism at specific occupational groups. One reads, for instance, that "the Church's failure to win the confidence of the technologist represents one of the most urgent problems facing it in modern society".

All that has been said about the mechanistic habit of considering human beings primarily in relation to their function is relevant here. It would be a surrender to secularist snobbery to imagine that the Church's failure to win the confidence of the technologist is any more significant or grave than its failure to win the confidence of the book-maker, the dustman, or the garage-hand. The Church's concern is with men and women as persons, not with technologists or bank clerks or miners as such. Anyone with parish experience knows that it is more important to the priest that Mr A is a husband and a father than that he is a technologist. It is more relevant to the parish priest that Mr A has a weak chest or a sunny disposition, or a pet dog, or a fondness for long walks, than that he is a technologist. It is more significant that he lives by the river, that he was born in Scotland, that he collects foreign stamps, and that he sings tenor, than that he is a technologist. Indeed, if we were to list in order the things about Mr A which really matter to the priest who is trying to convert him, then the fact that he is a technologist might well come comparatively low down on the list.

To the complaint that the Church is not getting into touch with technologists one must reply that the Church has a more important job to do — that of getting into touch with men and women, husbands and wives, grandparents and grandchildren, fiancés and their girl-friends, healthy men and sick men, cheerful women and sad women. Anything about them which is truly and richly human matters more than whether they earn their living as technologists or taxi-drivers.

In an age which increasingly classifies men and

women on a functional basis in relation to a dozen different machineries, social, economic, regional, it is essential that the Church should counteract this mechanistic bias. Every other agency in modern civilization tends to sub-divide us and categorize us into impersonal functional groupings. The Church, with its high conception of the human status, has other things to concentrate on than the fact that I am a plumber or a solicitor and you are a butcher or a typist. The Church deals with us as human beings. Especially it plays down those distinctions which determine our so-called social status and minister to our petty snobberies. That is, in so far as the Christian mind still lives and stirs feebly within the Church. For the Christian mind, overwhelmed with our high calling as men and women to be built into the mystical Body, obsessed with our truly human needs in health or sickness, in worship or in penitence, will certainly decategorize us in more trivial aspects. The things to be insisted upon when salvation is at issue are things which link you and me with the duke and the tramp, the millionaire and the dustman. There are too many influences about us, as it is, trying to hide those things from us. A living Christian mind will resist those influences. It will block off the intrusion of thinking tainted with mechanistic pre-suppositions into the life of the Church.

6

ITS SACRAMENTAL CAST

THE CHRISTIAN mind thinks sacramentally. The Christian Faith presents a sacramental view of life. It shows life's positive richnesses as derivative from the supernatural. It teaches us that to create beauty or to experience beauty, to recognize truth or to discover truth, to receive love or to give love, is to come into contact with realities which express the Divine Nature. At a time when Christianity is so widely misrepresented as life-rejecting rather than life-affirming, it is urgently necessary to right the balance. Especially is this the case where the young are concerned. Under the umbrella of current secularism, the body and its pleasures are being affirmed in an undisciplined cult of self-indulgence, unashamedly hedonistic. In denouncing excesses of sensuality, Christians are apt to give the impression that their religion rejects the physical and would tame the enterprising pursuit of vital experience.

There is no doubt that commercial interests actively stimulate youthful sexuality and self-indulgence. In short, men are making money out of corrupting the next generation. If there were a living Christian mind in the Church to-day, ecclesiastical authority would be pointing to these men, and would no doubt be excommunicating those of them who are officially practising Churchmen. (Meantime it would be interesting to discover by research how many men who are active in

Church affairs, and even at a high level, are themselves involved directly or indirectly in one of those industries whose publicity plays its part in seducing the souls of the young.) Instead ecclesiastical authority turns its guns on the easier target—the young victims of sex-obsessed advertisement, entertainment, and journalism. Since the young are unlikely to be contributing much to the propping up of medieval cathedrals, this is perhaps a more prudent course than taking on big business.

However that may be, it is plain that the religion of the Incarnation must be presented to modern youth as something more exciting than a lot of prohibitions aimed at disinfecting life of its torrential delights, and something more positive than a plan to substitute a sterility of body and mind for that contemporary fleshly abandonment which, if no longer glad, is at least per-versely affirmative of existence.

Youth is romantic. One of the manifestations of youth's romanticism is its sharpened sexuality. Consider the authoritative educative influences which play upon youth in this connection. Current secularism has not neglected the psychological and physiological back-ground of youth's acute sexuality; but it has naturally ignored the spiritual and theological significance. In secularist sociological and educational thinking, youth's potent aspirations, youth's profound glimpses of the wonderful, are treated as of essentially subjective psychological significance. On the other hand, the Church has presented to youth the Christian ethic and the Christian doctrines of redemption and salvation. But as for the meaning of youth's keen responsiveness to beauty and love, in this matter the Church has too readily handed over the young to be instructed by materialistic psychologists and amoral aesthetes. Yet, if

174

the Christian faith is not shown to touch the young at the points of profoundest personal longing and joy, it will indeed be condemned by the sensitive adolescent as being unrelated to real life.

A living Christian mind would elucidate for the young a finely articulated Christian sacramentalism which would make sense of, and give value to, the adolescent's cravings towards the grandeur of natural scenery, towards the potent emotionalism of music and art, and towards the opposite sex. A living Christian mind will not be content to refer to these things only in cold abstract terms which annihilate wonder and transmute them into bloodless modes of experience, unrecognizable as the stuff of passion and exaltation. Nor will the Christian mind allow these richnesses of life to be vaguely identified with the sins of the flesh, or even with a life of the body which it is the Christian's duty to transcend.

There are, I suppose, two departments of intellectual study in which the more educated modern adolescent is likely to find his deeper experiences seriously reckoned with. He may see them handled by the psychologist; or he may see them through the eyes of the poet. The psychologist, by the very nature of psychology, tends to reduce the significance of youth's romantic experiences to the physical level. Aspiration, love, and delight are presented in terms of appetite and sensation. This limited interpretation does scant justice to the spiritual aspect of youth's passions, and provides no sound basis for moral guidance. Moreover it tends to develop a self-conscious and calculated attitude to one's personal experiences of pleasure, which provides a convenient foundation for cynicism, self-indulgence, and insensitive exploitation of others.

The poet does greater justice to youth's romanticism. But if one considers the particular poets generally studied in schools and universities as typifying the kind of cultural influence which takes cognizance of adolescent romanticism, one is bound to have reservations about the healthiness of this influence. No doubt our popular poets do full justice to youth's dreams and desires in terms of sheer force and clarity of representation. They serve youth well in illustrating man's far-reaching potentialities for the experience of beauty and love. But too few of our poets are capable of referring their recorded raptures and agonies to a transcendental theory of life's meaning which is rationally acceptable and spiritually nourishing. There are notable exceptions of course, but many of our influential poets and writers generally lack a coherent philosophy of life's meaning. It is not being suggested here that it is necessarily the duty of a poet or writer to inculcate views of any kind. Our direct concern is with the kind of influences playing upon the minds of the young, and with the particular question how far we are providing the young with a theological framework to which their emotional experiences are relevant. Obviously, in the absence of a Christian mind, live and mature enough to provide the young with a view which subsumes all youth's moving experiences under the doctrine and discipline of the Faith, we hand over the young to alien influences at an impressionable and profoundly significant point.

Because youth is romantic, an articulate Christian Romanticism must be made available for them.

Perhaps it is necessary to justify romanticism itself, as an artistic fact, before making free with the phrase *Christian Romanticism*, which to some may smack of absurdity, to others perhaps even of blasphemy. To

176

many people the Classical principle in the arts would seem to be more in keeping with the Christian spirit than the Romantic principle. This is because the Classical principle comprehends ideas of order, poise, and temperate restraint, while the Romantic principle is regarded as comprehending lawless individualism and intemperate self-abandonment to the vagaries of personal fantasy and passion. The antithesis thus stated is unfair to the Romantic principle. It is true that Classicism stands for order, poise, and temperate restraint — for the control of individual fancy and vision in the interests of harmony and reason. But the artistic order and harmony for which Classicism stands presuppose the possibility of achieving a stability and perfection at the terrestrial level which the Christian regards as impossible of attainment within the finite. The Classical spirit in art proclaims by implication that man can achieve on earth representations of beauty and harmony which are wholly satisfying to him. The Classical spirit in music, art, architecture, and literature, is represented in the supposed attainment of forms whose beauty is a completeness, a completeness which offers serenity and satisfaction to the soul of man.

The Romantic principle is far different. It gives rein to individual fantasy and passion to a degree which opens the door to lawlessness, intemperance, and disorder. But the door which opens to lawlessness, intemperance, and disorder, offers at the same time a clear path to the exploration of limitless yearning and aspiration. In opening this door, Romanticism virtually proclaims that there is no final and complete satisfaction for man within the finite. The rejection of the Classical spirit is the rejection of the possibility of achieving stability and perfection at the terrestrial level. The assertion of

177

Romanticism is that man's profoundest yearnings and aspirations break beyond the bounds of any principle of order or harmony that can be fully manifested within the finite. The works and lives of great Romantic artists, if they testify to nothing else, certainly testify to the Christian belief that man is tortured and delighted by dreams and longings which earthly experience can never realize or set at rest. It is true that few Romantic artists have sensed the full significance of the yearnings which they have nursed and glorified, teased, sharpened, and even worshipped; but this failure in understanding does not invalidate the fundamental Romantic principle that it is right for man to fling his heart to the stars when the inner inspiration cries out for a reality beyond the scope of human fashioning. Instead this failure, like the current distorted romanticism of jiving, sex-ridden, gang-minded teenagers, stands as a challenge to Christian thinkers that they should touch man with the guidance and penetration of a theology at the point where his whole soul cries out that earthly life is not enough. And surely this cry is implicit in the rebellion of the delinquent teddy-boy or of the more educated but nonetheless amoral student, as it is in the tortured self-explorations of a Berlioz or a Baudelaire.

If we do not sympathize with romanticism, we do not sympathize with youth. If the Church does not reckon with romanticism, it does not cater for the young.

Strange longings are stirred in us by the grandeur of natural scenery, by the beauty of music and art, by the eyes and voice of the lover or the beloved. The general belief is that in youth these longings are most profound and perturbing. Whether this is true or not, it is certain that in youth these longings are accompanied by raptures and excitements which the more mature in years

178

are sadly incapable of recapturing. In youth these longings are themselves a keen delight, so that the young
will sometimes listen contentedly to those who tell
them that aspiration is more wonderful than achievement, the dream more joyful than the reality. In age the
longings, once so delightful, lose their edge; they
become tinged with melancholy and even with bitterness, as the sorrowful truth is grasped that beauty fades
and love grows cold, that music and art can cease to
captivate, that friends die and that life is short. When
longing loses its flavour, it is sad to have to believe that
longing itself is the heart of joy, and the image of fulfilment an idle fantasy. When dreams are no longer
stirred in us by mountain peaks or by passionate sym-
phonic movements, by the sweep of a girl's hair or the
falling of her eyelids, it is melancholy to have to believe
that the dreams themselves are the truest delight we are
to taste, and that the reality they seemed to mirror is a
fiction of the beguiling brain.

The alternative is to believe that longing is only
longing after all, that the dream is only a dream, but that
fulfilment and satisfaction remain, as ever, an offering
to man from beyond the world. And this, of course, is
the Christian view. It is also the common-sense view.
If the dreams and longings of youth did not lose their
edge and their delight, but moved to culmination in a
final, though finite, satisfaction, we should have less
cause to know our homelessness on earth. *Because* they
lose their intrinsic joy, we know our early dreams and
longings for what they are, the pointers to fulfilment and
reality; not ends in themselves, but significant disturbers
of our peace. Unsatisfied longings must be nourished in
us, and the elusive dream of fulfilment dangled before
us, or we should never know that we are not here, on

179

earth, in our proper resting-place. Utterly divested of this disturbing inheritance, men's hearts would never desire the ultimate peace and joy offered by God.

The Christian mind makes sense of passionate youthful longings and dissatisfactions as pointers to the divine creation of man and the fact that he is called to glory. Youth is constitutionally hungry to envelop with religious significance the yearnings aroused by natural beauty, by artistic experience, and by sexual love. Because there is no living Christian mind to interpret this hunger and to show how it may be fed, the young are led astray. False idolatries are enthusiastically pursued. The cult of the pop-singer is a plain instance of perverted romanticism. The pop-singer, as a symbol of the dual pull exerted by music and by sex, supplemented by the appeal of "artistically" heightened quality in physique, posture, dress, and movement, becomes the recipient of a homage religious in its depth and comprehensiveness, the object of a worship religious in its blend of personal devotion and collective ritual. At a less popular level false idolatries of another kind emerge. There is the artistic cult of uninhibited personal creativeness, spontaneity, and originality, which breeds amoral "religious" devotion to intemperate neurotic personalities. It was an idolatry of this kind which destroyed Dylan Thomas; and many others, artists and idolators alike, have suffered from the spuriously sanctified cultivation of eccentricity and excess. And no less dangerous, though far less feared by the respectable, is the false "religion" of love which dominates much contemporary fiction and journalism of an ostensibly innocuous kind. One does not need to turn many pages in the fiction library or on the magazine stall to find evidence of a dangerous doctrine. The shallow conception of mysterious eroticism triumphant over morality, convention, and restraint, is glamorized by the bogus sacredness of a perverted religiosity, which does not hesitate to abuse the traditional vocabulary of chivalrous romanticism and even of Christian morality.

Our thesis here is that the cult of the pop-singer, the teenager's passion for jiving, the experimentation with sex and drugs, the gangs and the violence, all express a perverted youthful romanticism. This romanticism is built of human longings neither more nor less valid than those which send masses of teenagers converging on youth hostels or on the Albert Hall for the Promenade concerts. We cannot cater for this romanticism by a programme for youth designed to disinfect it of passion, adventure, and sexuality. Nothing is now more dismally and tragically out of date than the Public School conception of the young man making his sterilized, clean-limbed way through life, shoulder to shoulder with all the other good types who wear short pants and play the game.

The Christian mind recognizes that youth's instinct to envelop experiences of music, sex, and communal adventure, with deep, passionate significance is fundamentally healthy. Youth's tendency to idealize—even to idealize the pop-singer and the film-star—springs from the instinct to spiritualize earthly experience, which is part of redeemed mankind's divine endowment. It is therefore logical and necessary that the fact of youthful romanticism should be subsumed into the theology of divine creation, incarnation, redemption, and salvation. But it is unfortunately more common in the educational world to find youthful romanticism interpreted in Platonic terms than in specifically Christian terms. This is one of the legacies of that nineteenth-century Public School ethos in which triumphant secularism masqueraded – and still masquerades – as Christian. It is not enough to present experiences of earthly beauty and love as glimpses of a reality beyond time. One must get beyond the cerebral and the abstract. There is need of the sense of personal inheritance, personal obligation, and personal vocation in relation to all that life offers to youth. Only the personal God can answer this need. Wordsworth's philosophic adoration of a Deity whose hand is on the morning hills is not enough. Nor is Browning's joyous exaltation in a sacramentally transfigured humanity. We need Coventry Patmore's devout acceptance of the God who woos the soul of man through the self-transcending grace of grateful love.

The Christian mind has a synthesis which theologizes the surly slum teenager's tortured instincts as readily as the fresh-faced, upper-middle-class Boy Scout's more comfortable ones. The Christian mind synthesizes in terms of God's demand and man's response. As it is in obedience to moral law and in progress in the spiritual life, so it is in the grateful and humble response to the pull of beauty in love, or art, or Nature. In all these instances it is the voice of God which calls, and the grace of God which urges us to listen. Youth's romanticism before the potent glamour of sex, music, dancing, and the like, must be a Christian romanticism which recognizes the divine Voice. Unless youth's stirring urges and visions are seen to point beyond time, they will be worshipped as ends in themselves. And so to worship them is to doom them. For, if they have not led beyond themselves when the time comes that they are granted more rarely, and finally not at all, their very reality will be questioned. They will be dismissed as subjective fantasies of the past or the outbreaks of repressed appetite and desire; and some sensitive souls will look back to them as evidence of Fate's trickery by which youth alone is made the happy and worth-while part of life. In any case mature age is likely to be tortured by backward searchings of regret and disillusionment, and by frustrated attempts to recapture what is gone. There is much of this in the poets. At a less sophisticated level, there is no doubt much of this too in the careers of criminals.

In no field of experience does secularism more insidiously drag man towards a sub-human level of living than in that of sexuality. The impulses towards idealization by which sexual love ought to be spiritual-ized and stabilized are perverted into means of glamoriz-ing passion at the expense of responsibility, duty, and charity. We have turned our attention to youth especi-ally here, partly because the damage done to youth by secularism's commercial and hedonistic exploitation of sexuality is particularly grave, and partly because the excesses and indiscipline of teenagers are catching the public eye and raising doubts even in minds wholly rooted in secularism. Having said that, one must add, speaking with philosophical detachment, that it is doubtful whether the teenage problem is anything more than a reflection of the general moral and spiritual decadence of society, for which of course the old always bear more responsibility than the young.

We have tried to put the teenage problem into a theological setting by seeing teenage excesses—in idolatry, sexuality, and abandonment to dance and music, for instance—as perversions of valid impulses rooted in human spirituality. God calls; and all the vehicles of natural and human beauty are at his disposal in tugging at the soul of man with the vision of the glory. Man responds; and all the richnesses of human

183

appetite, thrust, and aspiration are at his disposal in either answering obediently or answering rebelliously. He may submit to the discipline inherent in each call to taste and see, making of all things an offering and a self-dedication. Or he may assert the predominance of the grasping, enjoying self in a riot of claimed and plumbed indulgences. The one way leads to peace; the other way to torment.

Whilst Christians have been aware of this pattern of demand and response in the moral sphere and in the spiritual sphere, its relevance to such things as human sexuality, or experience of beauty in art and Nature, has been largely ignored. This is because we lack a Christian mind. The field of discourse upon these rich areas of human experience has been left to the secularists. Some of them have trodden there with clinical irreverence. Others, like the poets, with greater reverence but with too little understanding. Hence the moving, sensitive, but eventually frustrating raptures of a Shelley. Hence too the grand gropings of Wordsworth, a melancholy monument to the ultimate dissatisfactions of Christian brinkmanship.

Charles Williams tried to fill the gap. He left behind him a comprehensive, illuminating, and orthodox Romantic theology which does justice to the spiritual significance of sexual love. Christians who are aware of the need to reconstitute a Christian mind able to cope with all human experience theologically, ought to consult his work, notably *He Came down from Heaven* and *The Figure of Beatrice*. For the following brief summary of the doctrine of romantic love I draw upon Williams, and also upon Vladimir Solovyev's *The Meaning of Love*, and Coventry Patmore's *The Unknown Eros* and *The Rod, the Root, and the Flower*.

When a man falls in love, he sees the beloved in an

184

idealized vision which to the rest of the world seems unjustified by the facts of the woman's character and appearance. The lover feels towards his beloved, thus idealized, a rapture of devotion, which seems to blend humility with exultation, self-giving with grateful receiving, in a joyful interchange of laughter and courtesy. What is the real significance of this vision and the mutual relationship which can emerge from it? Williams tells us that the lover sees his beloved as all men would see one another, and all things, had not man fallen from his state of original innocence. He sees his beloved as all men ought to see their fellow-men "in God". The relationship between lover and beloved which emerges is (at its best) the relationship of joyful giving and receiving which ought to join all men together. Already such relationships exist among the perfected in Heaven. And the archetype of such perfected relationships is the coinherence of the Three Persons of the Trinity.

Romantic love presents to the lover a vision of the beloved in glory — the glory which, in the life of Heaven, will clothe all living things. The glory is revealed in the flesh. This is the mystery which the Incarnation represents archetypally. To some this vision is granted, not through romantic love, but through the beauty of Nature. In each case the vision is not an end in itself. Its purpose is to inspire man to search and strive for that "pattern of the glory" which is already known in Heaven, and which ought to transfigure the life of earth. The beloved herself is not a perfection after which the lover should strive to pattern all things: to attempt to do so is idolatry and superstition. Nor is Nature, in another context, such a perfection. But the glory which clothes the beloved and Nature in the given visions is of that perfection which will be known eternally in God. The vision is transient, and any attempt consciously to preserve it in relation to a particular context is not likely to succeed; but its effect ought to be permanent—leading man to accept the discipline of trying to learn to know all people and things in God.

I hope I have fairly represented the drift of Williams's thinking. Of course other lines than these have been followed by Christians anxious to formulate a true interpretation of sexual love. For Coventry Patmore the lover's desire for the beloved reflects the desire of God for the human soul. The husband's union with his wife is, in some mysterious way, related to God's union of himself with humanity in the act of incarnation. That this is a dangerous line of thought cannot be denied. It is so dangerous that paraphrase ought not to be attempted of the many illuminating correspondences which Patmore images in *The Unknown Eros*. For Solovyev the meaning of love lies in the opportunity it offers to man for realizing another person as a living subject. This is the beginning of that escape from self-centredness which the Christian Faith challenges us to explore to the full. Immortality, which is the promise of Christianity, is meaningless in terms of most activities which occupy us in the life of time: the whole significance of political, military, or cultural activities is contained within time; to imagine these activities prolonged indefinitely is to transmute them into absurdities. But love can endure immortality. More than that, love *needs* immortality. Death is incompatible with love.

It would be foolish to suggest, even by implication, that the contemporary problems of teenage sexuality could be solved by compulsory evening classes introducing the young to the works of Charles Williams,

Coventry Patmore, and Vladimir Solovyev. Our purpose in drawing attention to writers who have thought christianly about sexuality is to show how little there is of such thinking and how desperately it is needed if a Christian mind is to be established. Nothing which is truly human is outside the scope of theological synthesis; and sex is perhaps the dominant human interest of our day. Yet we have largely surrendered the right to interpret and legislate for human sexuality to the secular establishment which ignores man's divine creation and supernatural vocation.

The fashion for giving sex instruction in schools, and the nature of that instruction, are symptomatic of the Church's abdication. This instruction is supposed to prepare the young for a life in which sexual experience will be harmonious and fulfilling; yet it is almost exclusively clinical and hygienically divested of emotional overtones. It is difficult to understand why detailed understanding of the physiology of sex should be supposed to be an assistance to the happy practice of monogamy, especially in the absence of any instruction in the nature of love. The implication conveyed by much contemporary sex instruction is that the physical processes and events in sexual relationships are the important elements, the proper direction of which will ensure satisfactory human relationships. By an odd irony, the consideration of sexual love on a purely physical level is regarded as clean and healthy so long as other factors in sexual relationships are not discussed. The clinical approach is supposed to ensure healthy consideration of a delicate subject. In fact this emphasis in schools can have bad results. An adolescent may learn of love in two environments with their respective emphases. He may learn the clinical approach to sex at school, and in the evening he may learn to supplement this know-how from the sordid eroticism of the cinema and the Press.

Sexual love is one of the most powerful openers of the human mind to the reality of the eternal, one of the most potent disturbers of human willingness to come to terms with materialistic secularism. For nothing in natural experience more universally touches the soul of man with the call to worship, to serve, to adore, that which is outside himself, with the hunger for an immortality spent in love and self-giving. As a lever to prise open the heart of man to the awareness of mystery and to the glimpse of glory, both rooted in eternity, sexual love is one of God's most efficient instruments. It is precisely because it is such a fine, keen-edged instrument that it can be abused and exploited on an enormous scale, as it is to-day. Every advertiser in the world knows that you have only to touch a sensitive man's eyes with lines and curves lyrical with sexual overtones, and you have won his attention. Fortunes are made by the exploitation of this sensitivity where it is sharpest and most readily manipulable—in the young. If the Christian Church has neither words of condemnation violent enough to match the blackness of this sin against our humanity, nor a theology balanced and comprehensive enough to reassert the value of sexuality in an altogether loftier dimension, then it surrenders its grip upon modern man at a point where his experience cries out to be illuminated and redeemed. What a hullabaloo was created because D. H. Lawrence affirmed sexuality in terms of genitals handled with tenderness and without shame! What an inspiration it might be if the Church could reaffirm sexuality—and all human potentialities for the experience of beauty—in terms of man's hunger for Heaven and God's bountifully showered foretastes of the glory!

POSTSCRIPT

NO ONE can think deeply about the issue investigated in this book without sensing the possible approach of a crisis in Western civilization of a kind that is not being publicly anticipated. For, nuclear disaster apart, increasing mass-education, alongside increasing material well-being and accelerating pursuit of it, is going to make secularism more consciously and articulately secularist (as it is already in Russia). And this in turn will challenge Christians to be more consciously and articulately Christian. The question is, will the Christians of the next fifty years, over against a strengthened secularism, deepen and clarify their Christian commitment in a withdrawn cultivation of personal morality and spirituality, thereby achieving the kind of uneasy co-existence which Church and State appear to have arrived at in Russia? Or will the Christians of the next fifty years deepen and clarify their Christian commitment at the intellectual and social levels too, meeting and challenging not only secularism's assault upon personal morality and the life of the soul, but also secularism's truncated and perverted view of the meaning of life and the purpose of the social order? It is not that one fears Christians of the future will capitulate. We know our own weaknesses too well to sit in hypothetical judgement on future contestants against what is likely to be an even more potent and

189

insidious secularism than we ourselves have to encounter. Rather one fears that by sheer tactical error
Christians in the West may be gradually manoeuvred
into the position of Christians in Russia, content to say
the best that can be said of a social system wholly and
professedly committed to godless materialism, and
meanwhile sincerely keeping alive the flames of faith
and piety and moral virtue among a remnant that is
tolerated so long as it holds back from any comprehensive criticism of the established system.

The subtle steps by which Christians in the West
might be gently and slyly manoeuvred into this position
have never been plainly defined. This is a worrying
matter; for the present climate of opinion makes it
impossible to avoid taking these steps without opening
oneself to charges of "bigotry", "dogmatism", "doctrinaire intolerance", and without incurring that most
crushing of all contemporary smears — that one is being
"holier-than-thou". It is scarcely surprising that we have
taken many steps already towards a withdrawn and
departmentalized Christian spirituality severed from
contemporary culture by the drugged inoperancy of
the Christian mind. We shall take more such steps,
under the influence of that habit of settling down
quietly, if sometimes uncomfortably, with social
corruptions and intellectual perversions which cannot
be touched or condemned because good men and
fellow-Christians are involved in running or promulgat-
ing them, or because the political party which we
support as a bulwark against tyranny and materialism
has instructed us that these things are all right.

The time has come at which Christians must take the
initiative in order to avoid being outmanoeuvred. What
is demanded of us by the voice of the Church, if

properly understood, is likewise dictated by tactical and prudential considerations. In short, it is better to define, establish, and nourish a Christian mind in freedom now, as a positive last effort to bring light and hope to our culture and our civilization, than to have to try to gather together the miserable fragments of Christian consciousness after triumphant secularism has finally bulldozed its way through the Church, as a body of thinking men and women.

THE CHRISTIAN MIND
STUDY GUIDE

The Christian Mind presents a fresh and stimulating way of thinking that can help us view all areas of life in the light of Christian truth. Based on observations drawn from the author's study and contact with other Christians, the book contends that apart from questions of strictly personal morality, Christians today have adopted a secular way of thinking about political, cultural, social, and other important issues. As a result, the Church's ability to carry out an effective and fruitful mission in the modern world is gravely weakened.

Harry Blamires lucidly articulates the problem: "a withdrawn and departmentalized Christian spirituality severed from contemporary culture by the drugged inoperancy of the Christian mind" (p. 190). He also points the way to a solution—not by proposing a Christian approach to *specific* issues but by describing some of the elements that must characterize how Christians are to think about *every* issue. The two chapters that form part one of *The Christian Mind* explain and explore the deficiency; the six chapters in part two—each one focusing on a specific trait—illustrate what the Christian mind is.

The purpose of this study guide is to help readers of *The Christian Mind* to grasp the author's ideas, think them through, and apply them in their own lives. The guide contains nine studies, two for the first (and longest) chapter of *The Christian Mind,* and one for each subsequent chapter.

Each study is divided into three parts: "Take Aim" zeroes in on the main point or goal to be considered; the "Review and Reflect" questions ensure that the chapter's main ideas are understood; "Take Stock" invites readers to think about the material in terms of their own personal lives and to respond.

This study guide lends itself to both personal and group use. Here are a few suggestions that apply in either case:

1. You might read *The Christian Mind* in its entirety and then return to it as you work through the study guide. Or you can use the guide chapter by chapter, while reading the book for the first time.

2. Give yourself enough time to reflect on all the questions. They will take you through the chapter's main points, so you will benefit the most if you take time to answer each one. Some questions can be answered briefly and objectively by referring back to the book. Others solicit an opinion or invite further reflection. The "Take Stock" questions help you examine your life in light of the material just studied. If one session is not enough for a particular study, return to it in the next.

3. You may want to write down your answers in a notebook, or use a journal to keep track of ideas that catch your attention.

One last suggestion: pray. Acquiring a Christian way of thinking is not something we can do on our own. A book like *The Christian Mind* can expose a problem, convict us, give us the desire to change, and point out the ideal. But without the Holy Spirit at work in us, we cannot develop a Christian outlook on all of life or even recognize where our thinking has gone wrong.

So invite the Holy Spirit into your study of *The Christian Mind*. Ask him to open your eyes and heart. Use the "Take Stock" questions as a springboard for prayer. Be open to God's action. Ask God to use your efforts to bring you ever closer to the goal to which St. Paul urged the Christians of Rome:

> Do not be conformed to this world, but be transformed by the renewing of your minds, so that you may discern what is the will of God—what is good and acceptable and perfect.
>
> ROM 12:2

PART ONE
THE LACK OF A CHRISTIAN MIND

. Chapter 1 (pp. 3-43): The Surrender to Secularism

Take Aim: To understand what a Christian mind is, and why it is at the same time so rare and so critically needed today.

Review and Reflect:

1. Blamires states the problem in the opening sentence and expands on it throughout this chapter. What does he mean by "a Christian mind"? What characterizes "the *thinking* Christian"?

2. What charge does Blamires level at most Christians (p. 4)? How easy is it to think about secular issues in a Christian way?

3. Blamires contends that most of the insightful, influential critiques of our secularist culture—whether works of sociology or of imaginative literature—come from writers who are outside the Christian tradition. For what two reasons is this a problem?

4. Who would you add to Blamires' selection of writers who are prophetic voices protesting abuses in twentieth-century society?

   Are you surprised at some of his choices? What criteria might he be using?

5. Pages 11 to 12 describe the intellectual schizophrenia that besets today's thinking Christian. Do you think this is as big a problem as Blamires indicates it is?

6. Take some time to reflect on the relative absence of Christian thinking about secular issues in other branches of the media: TV and radio, movies, newspapers....

7. What price do Christians pay if they fail to communicate with one another as thinking beings? What does Blamires mean by "the loneliness of the thinking Christian" (p. 13)? Are you willing to try his experiment (p. 14)?

8. Why does Blamires insist that we need Christian "fields of discourse" to guide our thinking about secular issues (pp. 16-17)?

9. Blamires criticizes various aspects of British culture which prize superficial harmony and nurture a negative attitude towards ideas and ideals: an unreflective pragmatism (p. 18); a "sherry party" standard of trivial conversation (p. 19); the cultivation of "amusing" persons who have "something to say" about everything (p. 20). In what ways does American culture likewise discourage serious thinking?

10. What does this mean: "We have emptied political action of moral content" (p. 21)? Why does it matter?

11. Why does Blamires argue that loyalty may be "the key problem of our age" (p. 23) and that "it does enormous damage to our moral fibre" (p. 24)? How can loyalty make us complacent?

12. Blamires paints a bleak picture of thinking Christians caught up in secular institutions whose aims they deplore but are powerless to change. Do you agree with his assessment? How does he say this situation has come about?

13. Can you think of any areas of *personal* morality where a "full and lively Christian dialogue" is now being carried on? (See Blamires' example, p. 28.) If so, do you think today's dialogues effectively communicate the difference between secular and Christian thinking on these subjects?

14. Blamires brings Christian thinking to bear on two topics from the arena of public life. Review his remarks about advertising on pages 28 to 32. What can you learn from Blamires' approach? Do you find some of his questions outrageous (pp. 30, 32)?

15. Repeat the above exercise with Blamires' second topic, nuclear war (pp. 32-36).

16. What do you think is "the proper instrument for weighing, analyzing, and evaluating the secular world" (p. 39)? Why?

17. How can a misguided conception of Christian charity lead Christians to abdicate their responsibility to uphold the truth?

18. How does Blamires counter the objection that there *are* some contemporary books which present Christian thinking on secular issues?

19. Reading between the lines, what do you think is Blamires' purpose in writing this book? To whom is it primarily addressed?

Take Stock:
— Do I apply Christian thinking to most areas of life, or do I relegate it to issues of personal morality and spirituality?

— Have I ever experienced the intellectual schizophrenia or loneliness that Blamires describes? If yes, on what occasions?
— Do I understand what it means to have a Christian mind? Do I *want* to grow as a thinking Christian?
— Do I ever consider the ways in which I must necessarily participate in secular institutions with non-Christian aims? Does this leave me feeling frustrated? indifferent? resigned? Have I become too comfortable with the way of compromise?
— "We have manufactured a false 'charity' of the mind, which never takes a stand, but continually yields ground" (p. 39). Can this be said of me?

Chapter 2: Thinking Christianly
and Thinking Secularly

Take Aim: To grasp the difference between thinking in a Christian way and thinking about Christian matters.

Review and Reflect:
1. What does Blamires single out as the distinguishing mark of Christian thinking?
2. On page 45, Blamires demonstrates how a person might think Christianly about the most mundane of objects, in this case a gas pump. Choose some other everyday item—a spoon, perhaps, or a birdbath—and try thinking Christianly about it along the lines he has described.
3. Why does Blamires maintain that much of the dialogue concerning ecumenism is marked by secular thinking? If you were to think Christianly about ecumenism, how would your goal, tone, and line of reasoning differ from the secular thinker's? (See pages 46-47.)
4. Is it ever appropriate to think secularly?
5. "Perhaps never was there more secular thinking about things Christian" (p. 45), Blamires says of England as he writes, in 1963. And furthermore, "high-quality Christian thinking about the secular world" is "swamped by high-quality secular thinking about things Christian" (p. 49). Can this also be said of the U.S. in the nineties? Why might such a situation be a problem?

6. What does Blamires think is missing from the intellectual training of the British clergy? What are the effects of this deficiency?
7. What is the role of the thinker, or prophet, in the Church?
8. Blamires uses a lengthy example to illustrate the inability of people to think Christianly even about Christian matters: the English system of appointing bishops of the Anglican Church (pp. 52-62). In what ways does he contrast Christian and secular attitudes to: the adequacy of the current system, the bishop's function and position, the qualities that make for good bishops, mistaken appointments?
9. How is the misuse of Christian vocabulary—for example, the word "mystery"—a dangerous and destructive tendency of "wholly secular thinking" (p. 56)? Can you think of other Christian terms that have been similarly cheapened and distorted?

Take Stock:
— Is my thinking about secular everyday matters marked by an awareness of the eternal perspective, or is it mainly rooted in this world?
— Do I recognize myself in any of Blamires' descriptions of how the secular mind approaches Christian issues?
— Has this contrast of Christian and secular thinking revealed areas in which I need transformation? Am I willing to ask the Holy Spirit to show me where and how to change? In what other ways might I respond to what I have learned?

PART TWO
THE MARKS OF THE CHRISTIAN MIND

Chapter 1: Its Supernatural Orientation

Take Aim: To see that the eternal perspective of the Christian mind is meant to challenge secular thinking, not be undermined by it.

Review and Reflect:

1. In a nutshell, how would you contrast the Christian and the secular views of human life and history?

2. What is "the most basic presupposition of the secular mind" (p. 68)? How does it keep people from recognizing their creatureliness and dependence? from appreciating the Incarnation?

3. Blamires describes the "sly process" by which the Christian mind allows itself to be subtly secularized "by giving a purely *chronological* status to the eternal" (p. 69). What does he mean by this? What might prompt a Christian to choose this approach? Do you think the possible gains outweigh the consequences?

4. On pages 71 to 72, Blamires describes two ways in which many Christians act schizophrenic about their faith. Which does he consider the lesser of these two evils, and why?

5. How would you answer someone who insists that "whether I believe in an afterlife or not makes no difference to how I live today"?

6. Blamires holds that "the collision between the Christian mind and a solidly earthbound culture

ought to be a violent one" (p. 77)? Do you agree? What happens when such collisions are few?

7. In conversation one day a Christian and his secular neighbor discover that they are dealing with similar experiences: caring for an elderly parent with Alzheimer's disease; being promoted to a prestigious position; inheriting a fortune; learning that their unmarried teenage daughters are pregnant. Imagine what the secular-minded neighbor might say about each of these situations. How would an eternal perspective prompt the Christian to respond differently— in a way that his neighbor might find provocative and revolutionary?

8. Why does Blamires say that we Christians "have become afraid of our own convictions" (p. 84)?

Take Stock:

— Slowly read over the two descriptions of our world and the human situation on pages 73 to 74 and then ask yourself: Which description best captures my own view of life? Do I see myself as a fundamentally powerless creature or as an in-control, on-top-of-things, self-sufficient sort of person? Which view is fundamentally nearer to the truth?

— Blamires says that the Christian's supernatural orientation should confront secular thinking with "something to contend with: something different, something distinctive, something with depth, hardness, solidity; a pleasure to fight with and a joy to be beaten by" (p. 80). Do I encounter this quality in Christians I know? in Christians who are public figures? in myself?

Chapter 2: Its Awareness of Evil

Take Aim: To understand how the Christian mind views good and evil in the world.

Review and Reflect:

1. What is "the world" (p. 86)?
2. The secular mind does not *ignore* the conflict between good and evil, Blamires points out; rather, it interprets the conflict in a distorted, self-serving way. How would you describe this approach? What happens when Christians accept this distorted interpretation?
3. Reflect on how, as a Christian, your awareness of the sin of pride should: affect your perception of good and evil; steer you away from smugness and ready condemnation of others; help you see that insidious evil often coexists with social respectability.
4. To illustrate the contrast that should exist between the moral judgments of the Christian and the secular mind, Blamires zeroes in on two "fashionable current conformities." What do you think of his characterization of remarriage after divorce as "serial polygamy"? Does his line of reasoning make sense to you?
5. What is Blamires' second example of a "current conformity" to be rejected by the Christian mind? What does he say makes a work of art or literature immoral?
6. Blamires has already taken aim at the misuse of Christian vocabulary (see pp. 55-56). Here he protests the exploitation and perversion of other words (pp. 100-102). Is Blamires being picky, or is there some-

thing serious at stake here? Would you agree or disagree that this is a problem?

7. "There is about the Christian mind a peculiar hardness.... [a] cultivated suspiciousness" (p. 102). What does this mean? Why are these desirable qualities?

8. For the Church's judgment on the world not to become complacent and superior, what attitudes must accompany it?

Take Stock:

— Consider some of Scripture's statements about the world: "Do not love the world or the things in the world" (1 Jn 2:15). "We know that we are God's children, and that the whole world lies under the power of the evil one" (1 Jn 5:19). "But take courage; I have conquered the world!" (Jn 16:33). Ask yourself: What is my attitude toward the world—am I afraid of it? seduced by it? unaware of its influence?

— What "fashionable current conformities" do I encounter in my everyday life? How am I dealing with these ideas and situations? Do I go along with the crowd? Do I do what it takes to develop a truly Christian outlook—praying, getting informed, thinking?

— Slowly read out loud Blamires' address to modern man (pp. 103-104), then ask yourself: What does this tell me about the prevalence of evil in the world? about our Lord's presence in the midst of it? Does this stir me to hope—for myself? for others? Do I want to work with Christ as his instrument for good?

Chapter 3: Its Conception of Truth

Take Aim: To perceive the unshakable nature of Christian truth as objective, authoritative, God-given.

Review and Reflect:

1. What danger is there in relying too heavily on man-in-the-street interviews and public opinion polls and surveys?

2. "The sense of an objective truth existing within the sphere of religion has been lost. Religious conviction is, for the secular mind, a matter of individual preference...." (pp. 108-109). Do you think Blamires is exaggerating? Have you encountered this attitude?

3. Why is it arrogant—even blasphemous—to treat the Christian faith as a sort of self-improvement program?

4. Blamires stresses that Christianity is a "religion of acts and facts," with a hard, rocklike quality (p. 111). What does he mean? How is this different from the secular view of Christianity?

5. When defending Christian doctrines, why is it crucial to bear in mind that they are not theories, but descriptions of facts? How does this shift the ground of argument?

6. What two-pronged response does Blamires say we should make when a critic protests, "I believe in God, but I see no need for the Church"? Using the same reasoning, how would you answer someone who finds the idea of hell "judgmental" and "naive"?

7. What is the problem with certain personal testimony books which describe their authors' long, intellectual

journey toward the Christian faith? Can everyone arrive at God's truth?

8. Blamires contends that it is "off-centre thinkers," "subjectively opinionated people" within the Church, "who tend to draw attention to themselves" (p. 128). What do you think of his argument? What does he point out as the tragic effects of this situation?

Take Stock:
— What comes to my mind when I hear the word "truth"? Where do I look for truth?
— Is the way I live my life founded on objective, divinely-revealed truth, or on personal opinion—my own and others'? What are my particular areas of weakness?
— Think about an occasion when you were challenged about your Christian beliefs. Have you learned anything from this chapter that might have helped you to make a better response?

Chapter 4: Its Acceptance of Authority

Take Aim: To examine why secular and Christian thinking are at odds in their approaches to authority and obedience.

Review and Reflect:

1. What are the only two possible choices that a person may reasonably make when confronted with Christian truth?

2. What do you think of Blamires' contention that our world is marked by "a distaste for authority unparalleled in history" (p. 133)? Is there a good side to this rejection? How are notions of authority and obedience crucial to Christian thinking and acting?

3. On pages 133-136 Blamires describes how people's experience of politicians and government agencies can warp their view of authority. Can you relate to his examples? Can you add to them?

4. "Father"—what two vital aspects of God should this word evoke for us? Why is it wrong to separate the two?

5. Think about the media portrayal of fatherhood in recent years; has it improved any since Blamires wrote?

6. In presenting issues related to Christian belief and behavior, what are some of the methods that secular thinkers, especially in the media, use to undercut the response of obedience?

7. How can a person's acknowledgment of God's existence be "rooted in the human urge to mastery" (p. 145)? How does the proud, unsubmissive mind view God

and the Christian faith—perhaps while at the same time calling itself "Christian"?

8. Why does Blamires say that the Christian thinker rightly reacts against the slogan, "The Church must adapt itself to the modern world" (p. 148)? How does he turn the argument around?

9. What is wrong with the pragmatic view that the Church is "a means of achieving something secularly worthwhile" (p. 150)?

10. What answer does Blamires propose we make to pessimists who paint the Church as a dying institution and ask, "Can the Church survive?" (p. 152)?

11. On the other side, what error about the Church's future might optimists fall into?

Take Stock:

— "Authority is something whose grip you grow out of, something you break away from. It is something you view with suspicion, something you combine against in order to limit its operations" (p. 139). To what degree has this secular way of thinking distorted my attitude toward the authority of God? of his revelation? his commandments? his Church?

— Reflect on your experiences of personal authority: with your parents, teachers, bosses, other authority figures. Have these encounters enhanced or undermined your ability to obey God?

— Do I relate to God as my Father who both loves me deeply and has complete authority over me? Do I need his healing and help in this area? Will I turn to him for what I need?

Chapter 5: Its Concern for the Person

Take Aim: To understand how technology can shape everyday life and thinking in ways that depreciate the human person and seduce us from the service of God.

Review and Reflect:

1. What does it mean to say that Christian thinking is incarnational?
2. Blamires points to the car as a prime example of some people's tendency to let machines control their lives. Do you find his reasoning persuasive? How would you apply it to the other areas he mentions: TV, radio, the movies? What other conveniences are likely to be stumbling blocks today?
3. What are some of the dangers of seeking "the good life" in the acquisition of material possessions?
4. Who does Blamires see as the exploiters and the exploited in modern society? With what does he reproach Christians in this regard?
5. In what ways does slavery to technology work against a Christian way of thinking? Why is it wrong to view people mainly in terms of their functions?
6. On pages 163-166, Blamires describes how secular thinking leads us to see various organizations as "machines" (he zeroes in on the educational system as an example). Have you ever felt this way about any of the organizations—social, financial, political, cultural, religious—to which you belong? Why?
7. What is the difference between an institution and a mechanism? Where does the Church fit in?

8. When one allows mechanistic thinking to seep into the Church, Blamires contends, "one reverses the Christian mission" (p. 168). What does this mean?

9. "The Church deals with us as human beings" (p. 172). Why is this the basis for authentic evangelism? How does this differ from evangelistic attempts which stem from a mechanistic, functional view of the human person?

Take Stock:

— What does it mean to me that "the Word became flesh and lived among us" (Jn 1:14)? Does the Incarnation affect the way I think about others? about myself? What could I do to open myself more fully to this reality?

— What is my ideal of "the good life"? Do I make good choices about buying and using the various conveniences of modern life? How does advertising affect me?

— "We know, as Christians, that our calling is to live as free, choosing, active men and women, making the best use possible of a world which is God's creation too" (p. 159). If I were more consistently conscious of this calling, what would I change about the way I live?

— Have Blamires' insights revealed any ways in which my view of the Church has been affected by secular thinking?

Chapter 6: Its Sacramental Cast

Take Aim: To consider how a sacramental view of life enriches our physical experience by explaining and directing our desires for truth, beauty, and love.

Review and Reflect:
1. What is a sacramental view of life? Without it, what do Christians lack?
2. Why do people—and especially *young* people—need not only the Church's presentation of sexual ethics but also its explanation of the spiritual significance of sexuality?
3. Blamires cites psychology and poetry as largely "alien influences" that shape young people's view of their romantic experiences (pp. 175-76). What perspective characterizes the psychologist's thinking about this area? With what results? What is the poet's message? Is it adequate?
4. Blamires distinguishes between the Classical and the Romantic principle in the arts. What characteristics of Classicism would lead some people to conclude that it is akin to the Christian spirit?
5. Why is Romanticism, not Classicism, more in keeping with Christian thinking? What great realities emerge even in the distorted romanticism of both artists and youth? What challenge to the Church?
6. How does the Christian mind explain the passions and yearnings that are stirred up by experiences of beauty, art, and love?

7. What is missing if such experiences are viewed only in an abstract, theoretical way? What personal message and response are they intended to evoke?

8. Blamires introduces three Christian thinkers who have sought to explain the spiritual meaning of sexual love: Charles Williams, Coventry Patmore, and Vladimir Solovyev (pp. 184-86). Does his brief presentation of their thinking suggest some fruitful new ways in which to consider the area of sexuality?

Take Stock:
— Am I stirred by the beauties of creation, great works of art, experiences of love? Do I recognize God's voice in these things, calling me to respond to him? Am I responding?

— Do I sometimes feel that Christianity is "no fun" and "just a lot of rules"? Has this chapter helped me to see where my view of the Christian faith might be deficient? How would I answer a young person who has the same objections about the faith?

— Am I familiar with the authors Blamires mentions at the end of this chapter? Might I benefit from exploring their thinking in greater depth?

— Take some time to reflect on your study of *The Christian Mind.* What have you learned? What practical effect will it have on the way you live? Commend your thinking to the Lord and ask him to continue teaching and forming you in this area.

CPSIA information can be obtained at www.ICGtesting.com
Printed in the USA
LVOW12s1131300914

406545LV00001B/58/P

9 781573 833233